DogLife ❖ Lifelong Care for Your Dog™

BOXER

tfh

Cynthia P. Gallagher

BOXER

Project Team
Editor: Stephanie Fornino
Copy Editor: Joann Woy
Indexer: Lucie Haskins
Design: Angela Stanford
Series Design: Mary Ann Kahn

T.F.H. Publications
President/CEO: Glen S. Axelrod
Executive Vice President: Mark E. Johnson
Publisher: Christopher T. Reggio
Production Manager: Kathy Bontz

T.F.H. Publications, Inc.
One TFH Plaza
Third and Union Avenues
Neptune City, NJ 07753
Copyright © 2010 TFH Publications, Inc.

Printed and bound in China

10 11 12 13 14   1 3 5 7 9 8 6 4 2

Library of Congress Cataloging-in-Publication Data

Gallagher, Cynthia P.

  Boxer / Cynthia P. Gallagher.

     p. cm.

  Includes bibliographical references and index.

  ISBN 978-0-7938-3602-4 (alk. paper)

  1. Boxer (Dog breed) I. Title.

  SF429.B75G348 2010

  636.73--dc22

                        2010002419

This book has been published with the intent to provide accurate and authoritative information in regard to the subject matter within. While every reasonable precaution has been taken in preparation of this book, the author and publisher expressly disclaim responsibility for any errors, omissions, or adverse effects arising from the use or application of the information contained herein. The techniques and suggestions are used at the reader's discretion and are not to be considered a substitute for veterinary care.

If you suspect a medical problem consult your veterinarian.

Note: In the interest of concise writing, "he" is used when referring to puppies and dogs unless the text is specifically referring to females or males. "She" is used when referring to people. However, the information contained herein is equally applicable to both sexes.

The Leader In Responsible Animal Care for Over 50 Years!®
www.tfh.com

CONTENTS

INTRODUCTION

INTRODUCING THE BOXER

Nobel Prize-winning French author Anatole France once said, "Until one has loved an animal, a part of one's soul remains unawakened." Substitute the word "Boxer" for "animal," and you have a maxim that Boxer lovers all over the world would consider grossly understated.

Every dog breed has its fanciers, but Boxer people are especially enthusiastic about the breed, and with good reason. Boxers are as intelligent, gentle, and lovable as they are handsome, powerful, and playful. They are great all-around family pets and perennial favorites in the show ring. To know them is indeed to love them, but to really know them, it helps to understand their past, present, and the possibilities in their future.

BRIEF HISTORY OF THE DOMESTICATION OF THE DOG

To look at today's Boxer, one wouldn't necessarily think that the endearing qualities of the breed have emerged from a group of breeds utilized hundreds of years ago for unsavory tasks like butchering and so-called "entertainments" like bear- and bullbaiting and dog-fighting. The Boxer's evolution as a breed is very recent compared to the long history of partnership between man and dog. *Homo sapiens* (modern man) existed as long ago as 90,000 years in the Middle East and 35,000 ago years in Europe. Recent studies suggest that the wolf (*Canis lupus*), generally acknowledged as the domestic dog's wild ancestor, diverged into a separate species about 100,000 years ago. Exactly when man and canine teamed up synergistically, no one is certain.

Dogs appeared in art as far back as 6500 BCE, when cave drawings depicted canine figures alongside humans. The jawbone of a domesticated dog dated to about 12,000 years ago was found in a cave in Iraq, providing significant evidence that dogs of that era differed from wolves, with smaller jaws and teeth. Because our knowledge of the Stone Age is limited, we don't know exactly when dogs and wolves separated into distinct species of the genus *Canis*. We do know that by 4000 BCE in Egypt (one of the world's oldest civilizations), dogs were friends and servants of humans, living in their houses, accompanying them on walks, and appearing with them in public ceremonies. We also know that ancient Roman civilization included dogs: The remains of a collared, chained dog, naturally preserved

Boxers are intelligent, gentle, and lovable.

by volcanic ash, was excavated from the ruins of the unfortunate Italian city of Pompeii, destroyed by the eruption of Mount Vesuvius in 79 CE.

During the most recent Ice Age (about 20,000 years ago), humans and wolves were significant predators with a lot in common. Both lived and hunted in family-based packs led by a dominant male whose female partner likely held authority second only to his own. This social system enabled both species to hunt animals far bigger than themselves. Therefore, a hunting partnership between wolves and early humans was natural and mutually beneficial, despite their competition for the same prey. Wolves benefited from human ingenuity and weaponry, resulting in a greater number of kills and larger-sized prey, like mammoth.

Humans benefited from canine speed and ferocity, essentially a new type of weapon. Their compatibility and the wolf's willingness to breed in human company established the partnership from which all dogs derive.

Selective breeding can affect a species quite rapidly, and it's only natural that man would develop a preference for a particular puppy and perpetuate his favored characteristics. Dogs began to develop into different shapes and sizes, for specific purposes (e.g., Roman ladies kept small lapdogs, thought to cure stomach upset). By the first century CE, a dog very like the modern Pekingese existed in China. In the same period, a Roman writer proffered practical reasons for selecting a dog's color: Herding dogs should be white to distinguish them from wolves in the dark, but farmyard dogs should be black to scare thieves. Thus were different breeds perpetuated, further distinguishing them from their wolf ancestors.

Some controversy exists over the global location of dog's domestication—some experts believe Africa, others think East Asia—but it is fair to say that every single dog breed evolved from the wolves who roamed side by side with their human hunting partners.

EARLY DEVELOPMENT OF THE BOXER

The Boxer as we know him today is a paradox: a relatively recent breed with ancient origins.

Ancient Origins

Earlier than 2000 BCE, the Assyrians bred a strain of powerful dogs with large, heavy heads and great courage, to be used in battle. A few hundred years later, this type of dog was named "Molossian," after the city of Molossis in Epirus (now Albania). Dog breeds in ancient times were not named as specifically as they are now; dog groups were typically named for the type of work performed or for the geographical region where they originated. Molossian dogs resembled Mastiffs, and their courage and tenacity were prized by warriors who went side by side with them into battle. So remarkable was their savage fighting ability

that one Egyptian pharaoh maintained 2,000 Molossian dogs in his army.

The Middle Ages

During the Middle Ages, mechanical armaments began to surpass the destructive power of the mighty Mastiff/Molossian dogs on the battlefront. But their strength and courage were not retired, simply redirected. Noblemen began utilizing dogs as guards and hunters of large marauders like bison, bears, and their own ancestors, wolves. The dogs' savage ability so impressed Europeans that they soon began to match them against other animals in mini-spectacles, and ultimately, in

The Boxer as we know him today is a relatively recent breed with ancient origins.

Germany early recognized the Boxer's breed potential.

that the ritual drew crowds. Soon they were pitting their bullbaiters against other village dogs in a macabre contest of savagery, observing that the dogs whose jaws were most undershot were able to maintain the longest bite hold, as their stubbed noses allowed free breathing while their jaws clamped the animal. The horrific "sport" of dog-fighting was born.

Bear- and bullbaiting flourished throughout Belgium and Germany, where audiences thrilled to the dogs' "gameness," or tenacity, that kept them baiting the large animal even when tossed 30 feet (9 m) in the air on the bull's horns or deeply gouged by the bear's deadly claws. The first "pit bull" dog breeds, *Bullenbeisser* (bullbaiter) and *Barenbeisser* (bearbaiter), emerged distinctive from their Molossian origins.

The More Modern *Bullen-* and *Barenbeissers*

These large *Bullen-* and *Barenbeissers* were fearless, but the very physiological structure that made them powerhouses in battle made them less than agile in the fighting pits. Many dogs perished in these encounters, leaving only the quickest dogs to dominate the gene pools. Natural selection replaced the Mastiff/Molossian dogs with smaller, faster descendants who became known in the fighting culture as "bulldogs." Although they little resembled today's Bulldogs, they were the forerunners of many breeds, including Boxers.

While the new bulldogs became established in blood sports throughout Europe during the 18th century, the Belgian city of Brabant became an active breeding center. The result

full-fledged sport. Fighting arenas throughout Europe "entertained" barbaric civilizations by pitting dogs against every sort of creature, from man to elephant.

Bull- and Bearbaiting

Bullbaiting was a cruel pastime with practical origins. Village butchers kept dogs to "bait" (bite) animals intended for slaughter because popular belief held that baited meat was more tender and nutritious. The bull or cow was restrained by a chain or rope while the unrestrained dog(s) repeatedly attacked it. Butchers, who used their own dogs, noticed was a smaller, more agile dog. Medium sized and well muscled, the *Brabanter Bullenbeissers* (BB) appeared similar to early English Bulldogs, who little resembled today's Bulldog.

Throughout the Low Countries and Germany, *Bullenbeissers* flourished as hunting dogs for the nobility. These dogs had an instinct for tackling game from behind and holding it for the hunters' arrival without incurring serious injury. The BB's powerful head and undershot jaw allowed the dog to keep breathing freely while maintaining a firm hold on the prey. Wrinkles and/or folds around the dog's nose acted as canals for the animal's blood to run off the sides of the dog's muzzle, avoiding his eyes. This feature remains quite pronounced in the modern Bulldog. The dog's ears and tail provided convenient bite holds for opponents and icurred particularly bloody wounds when ripped or torn. Dog owners usually cropped ears and docked tails to prevent injury during a hunting skirmish or staged fight.

Not surprisingly, these dogs were highly prized and meticulously bred. The *Brabanter Bullenbeisser* is generally accepted as the direct ancestor of the modern Boxer.

BREED HISTORY IN GERMANY

Germany has always prided itself in its role as a cultural and intellectual center, so its early recognition of the Boxer breed's potential is no surprise.

The Boxer's Role in Germany

When the Napoleonic Wars of the early 19th century disbanded the estates of those German noblemen who so highly valued their BB hunting companions, the dog's versatility really came to the forefront. They became firmly ensconced as family and guard dogs due to their high intelligence and trainability. They also became invaluable assistants to butchers and cattlemen, catching and holding fast the cow or bull for slaughter. Although less glamorous than hunting with nobility, the breeder's skill at such jobs ensured its perpetuity.

The same tenacity and gameness that made the BB useful professionally also rendered him a profitable commodity. The popularity of dog-fighting as "sport" had spread to England, where working classes had little in the way of hobbies or entertainment. Dog-fighting developed into a subculture taken very seriously by its proponents, who carefully and selectively bred a smaller, more agile dog than the pure BB. It is believed that in 1830, a BB was crossbred with that era's English Bulldog (who more resembled a small Mastiff than the Bulldog we know today), resulting in the modern Boxer.

Exports to Germany

In the late 1830s, England exported their new variety of *Bullenbeisser*/Bulldog/Boxer to Germany, where they kept meticulous breeding records. This dog appears twice in the pedigrees of early German Boxers, and provided genes that introduced the heretofore unknown white color to the *Bullenbeissers*. It's likely that the large head of this breed patriarch established the Boxer head standard.

Boxer breeders continue to endeavor to produce litters that conform most closely to the standard.

Official Breed Club

Although breeders and other enthusiasts frequently met, an official breed club was not formed until 1895, which is relatively recent considering how long ago dog and human first forged a relationship. The *Deutscher Boxer Klub* (German Boxer Club) was established in Munich, and other German clubs soon followed. How they decided on the breed name "Boxer" is more nebulous, however.

What's in a Name?

Contrary to popular belief, the Boxer did not get his name from an upright play stance, "boxing" with his front paws. Although the specific origin of the name is unclear, it isn't plausible that German breeders would have proudly named their new breed after a national British symbol like boxing. Historians and German linguistic experts believe the oldest written source for the breed name to be the 18th century German dictionary of foreign languages, *Deutsches Fremdwörterbuch*, in which the word *baxer* appeared. *Baxer* and *Boxer* are sufficiently similar to infer origin, but we'll never know for sure. Another theory suggests origin in the Bavarian word *boxl*, meaning "short leather trousers" or "underwear." A further idea is that the BB was known as the *Boxl*, and "Boxer" is a distortion of that word. Yet another explanation is that the English-language translation of the German word *boxer* is "prize fighter," and the Boxer was so named to acknowledge the fighting heritage he and his predecessors bore.

The Breed Standard

Once the *Deutscher Boxer Klub* was organized, it developed a breed standard to better define the physical and temperamental characteristics of the breed. The breed standard is the measurement of perfection against which all dogs of that breed are compared. Breeders continually endeavor to produce litters that conform most closely to the standard. Records from the first decades of the German Boxer Club indicate a dog who still looked quite different from today's elegant Boxer. Early Boxers had a thicker build and longer body, as portrayed in a surviving photograph of contestants in the club's first show. Even today, Boxers bred in Germany differ slightly from those bred in the United States, with a thicker skeletal structure and a little larger head. If you examine the first few generations' pedigrees in early 20th-century Germany, it's clear that a good deal of inbreeding took place. Setting the genetic foundations of a new breed cannot be accomplished in any other way.

The Matriarch of the Boxer in Germany

A truth universally acknowledged is that the human matriarch of the modern Boxer in Germany was a breeder named Friederun Stockmann (1891–1972). Along with her husband Philip, Frau Stockmann ran the vom Dom ("of the cathedral") Kennels and swiftly developed uniformity within the breed and closer conformation to its standard. In her book *My Life with Boxers*, Frau Stockmann describes the effect World War I had on Germany's Boxers. Philip Stockmann trained and placed Boxers as war dogs with the German army, taking ten Boxers with him to the front lines. Only one returned. The dogs who remained at home suffered from the same food shortages as the German people. Frau Stockmann went to Herculean lengths to find food for her Boxers, a problem exacerbated by the postwar economic inflation. The Boxer population in Germany, already severely reduced by the war, decreased even further afterward. Of the Boxers who survived the war, many proved sterile, and a high mortality rate affected litters that were produced.

The Boxer was originally assigned to the Non-Sporting Group but was eventually reassigned to the Working Group.

The Boxer is recognized by a variety of professional dog breed clubs around the world, including the American Kennel Club (AKC).

Just as German breeders were beginning to overcome these genetic anomalies, World War II began. Boxers once again became war dogs, whisked away by the German government and usually never seen again by their owners. However, passing the rigorous tests on which acceptance as a war dog was predicated guaranteed regular food for these canine conscripts. And in a time of severe food shortages throughout Europe, this meal ticket eclipsed the dangers of warfare.

It would take three long years after World War II ended before the German Boxer would recover from the acute disruption to his development as a breed and resume his place as one of the country's most exceptional dogs.

HISTORY OF THE BOXER IN THE UNITED STATES

There's a certain symmetry to the fact that the first Boxer to gain recognition by the American Kennel Club (AKC) in 1904 came from Frau Stockmann's vom Dom Kennels. Eleven years later, a Boxer named Dampf v. Dom, owned by New York Governor and Mrs. Herbert H. Lehman, finished his American championship. Because there were relatively few Boxer bitches in America, Dampf v. Dom had few requests for stud service, and it would take another 15 years for the rest of the United States to catch Boxer fever. In the early 1930s, imported German champion Boxers campaigned at AKC shows, captivating dog enthusiasts.

As US familiarity with the breed grew, and as more and more Boxers won the coveted Best in Show title, the breed's popularity flourished. Other vom Dom Boxers came and conquered, winning titles and setting records. Four dogs in particular became known as the foundation of Boxers in America: Sigurd, Dorian, Utz, and Lustig. Sigurd, grandfather of the other three, was recognized for many years as a leading sire in the United States.

Official Breed Club
In May 1935, the AKC approved the establishment of the breed's parent organization, the American Boxer Club (ABC). Initially, Boxers were placed in the Non-Sporting Group, one of the seven distinct categories in which all AKC-recognized breeds fall. The fledgling ABC, with only 17 members at first, felt the classification inadequate to the Boxer's versatility, and successfully petitioned the AKC to reassign the breed to the Working Group, where it remains today.

The Breed Standard
The breed standard proved problematic in the early days of the ABC. The one in use at that time was an English translation of a pre-1920 German standard or an even older Austrian version. Therefore, the first breed standard adopted by the ABC was not the current German standard. This meant that the Boxers imported into the United States from Germany, and their progeny, did not conform to the US standard. Herr Philip Stockman came to the rescue in 1938, helping to revise the breed standard while serving as Boxer judge at that year's Westminster Kennel Club's prestigious show. The newly adopted standard matched more closely the contemporary German Boxer standard.

America's Love Affair With the Boxer
Even as World War II loomed, America continued its love affair with the Boxer, mirroring what Germany already had known for some time. Many notable Boxer kennels evolved during this period, but perhaps none enjoyed the celebrity of the Sirrah Crest Kennels. Established in 1939, by Dr. and Mrs. R.C. Harris, who desired to become serious Boxer breeders ("Sirrah" is "Harris" spelled backward), Sirrah Crest's breeding program began with two puppies purchased from another noteworthy American kennel of the 1930s, Mazelaine, whose owner John Wagner had many litters of champions descending from the "Great Four" Boxers.

Boxers are great all-around family pets.

In 1949, Sirrah Crest earned its place in the annals of Boxer breeding with the birth of a flashy fawn male named Bang Away. His conformation career began at the age of two and a half months, when he was named Best in Match at a local puppy show. Serendipitously, the show was judged by none other than Frau Stockmann, who predicted that Sirrah's Bang Away would become America's greatest Boxer. And he did—winning 21 Best in Show titles (including Westminster) in six years. He sired generations of champions and dramatically increased the Boxer's popularity in the United States. The striking elegance and grace he demonstrated year after year continues to reflect in America's top Boxers today.

Recognition of the Boxer Breed

The Boxer breed in the United States developed apace with the concept of breed organizations to standardize serious dog breeding. There are many professional dog breed clubs around the world; a few are more familiar than others.

American Kennel Club

The AKC is the oldest and most influential multi-breed dog club in the United States. Founded in 1884, it oversees the member clubs of individual breeds, making it a "club of clubs." The AKC serves a number of purposes: registration of purebred dogs, presidency over dog shows, and involvement in public awareness and legislation on all dog-related issues. The AKC also publishes the official standards for all recognized breeds and promotes responsible dog ownership.

In 1942, the AKC compiled an official list of recognized breeds and varieties. New breeds, like the Boxer, were required to form parent clubs and maintain their own registries prior to seeking AKC recognition.

American Boxer Club

The 1930s were a time of much growth in the US dog-breeding realm, as many individual breed clubs were formed. The ABC was organized by a group of New York City fanciers in February of 1935. With a roster of 17 members, they were granted AKC membership three months later. Their first order of business? A petition to reclassify the Boxer's breed group from Non-Sporting to the recently established Working Group. Their request was granted that September, and the Boxer remains a working breed to this day. Soon after, though, controversy over the club's official Boxer breed standard took center stage.

The neophyte ABC adopted an English translation of a pre-1920 German standard or an even older Austrian version. This meant that show Boxers imported into the United States from Germany, which had updated its breed standard, were judged against an obsolete US standard containing outdated and now undesirable traits. Herr Philip Stockmann solved the problem in 1938, by helping to revise the breed standard while serving as Boxer judge at that year's Westminster Kennel Club's show. The newly adopted US standard more closely matched the contemporary German Boxer standard. Further revisions lay ahead, the most recent of which came in 2005.

United Kennel Club

Although the AKC receives most of the publicity, it is not the only major dog registry in North America. The United Kennel Club (UKC) is the largest all-breed performance-dog registry in the world. Established in 1898, the UKC currently registers dogs from all 50 states and 25 foreign countries. While the AKC focuses on conformation and breeding, the UKC concentrates on a wide variety of events that support their "total dog" philosophy, which holds that the ideal dog is more than just a pretty face. Over 60 percent of the UKC's 1,300 licensed events test obedience, hunting ability, and instinct. The club prides itself on these family-friendly, educational events that embrace a dog's ability to perform as well as he appears.

The American Boxer Club was formed in 1935.

Other differences between the two clubs include the groups into which registered breeds are dispersed. There are similarities, but the UKC groups are more specific than their AKC counterparts. The UKC also recognizes more breeds than the AKC, some rarely seen outside the region where they originate, such as the Porcelaine, a scenthound from France's Normandy region, and the Akbash, a herding dog of western Turkey.

Memorable Boxers and Influential People

Such a relatively young breed as the Boxer could not have flourished in America without the influence of several pioneers.

The Stockmanns' vom Dom Kennels

Frau Friederun Stockmann is regarded as the most important figure in Boxer history. The superior dogs that she bred and her husband trained served the German war effort in World Wars I and II. Vom Dom Boxers are considered the cornerstones of all American Boxer pedigrees, as so many were exported to the United States, became champions, and bred future champions. Herr Philip Stockmann was instrumental in revising the early breed standard for the newly formed American Boxer Club.

Mazie and Jack Wagner's Mazelaine Boxers Kennel

Originally Great Dane breeders, the Wagners turned to breeding Boxers during the Hoover administration. Their first litter was sired by a German export, Sieger ("champion") Check v. Hunnenstein, who left his mark on generations of champions, including Ch. Dorian v. Marienhof, one of the "Great Four."

R.C. and Phoebe Harris' Sirrah Crest Kennel

When Dr. and Mrs. Harris decided in 1939 to become serious Boxer breeders, little did they realize that they would produce the most winning Boxer of the century. With two puppies purchased from Wagners' Mazelaine Kennel, they began a breeding program that yielded Bang Away of Sirrah Crest in 1949. His iconic show career began with his first title of Best in Match at the tender age of two and a half months, awarded by the illustrious Frau Stockmann.

Governor and Mrs. Lehmann of New York

These Boxer fanciers helped establish the ABC and owned the first Boxer to finish an AKC championship, Sieger Dampf vom Dom, a German import from vom Dom Kennels.

James Welch of Illinois

This Boxer breeder/owner holds the distinction of producing the first Boxer to be registered with the AKC in 1904, Arnulf Grandenz.

Other Notable Enthusiasts

Other notable Boxer enthusiasts include G.J. Jeuther, whose Boxer was the second in the United States to finish a championship; Dr. Benjamin Birk, who imported German Boxers as foundation breeding stock for his Birkbaum Kennels; Marcia and Joseph Fennessey,

whose Boxer became the third to finish a championship in the United States; and Henry Stoecker, whose Boxer was the first female champion in the United States and the first to be born in America. Through their efforts and that of other Boxer devotees, the breed has evolved into the statuesque, endearing dog we love to love.

PART I

PUPPYHOOD

CHAPTER 1

IS THE BOXER RIGHT FOR YOU?

2008 American Kennel Club (AKC) statistics indicate that the Boxer is the sixth most popular dog in the United States, and with good reason. Few breeds have the versatility that is inarguably the Boxer's best quality. He can adapt to various living environments, can perform well at almost anything, makes as superior a watchdog as he does a family companion, and loves all types of humans. He is an irresistibly endearing puppy who grows into a strikingly handsome adult dog. But before you capitulate to the siren call of a Boxer pup, you need to closely examine your lifestyle to determine if it is compatible with a Boxer's needs and wants. It's often hard to reconcile the soft, warm bundle in your arms with the tall, energetic powerhouse he will become—and soon. A Boxer enters "adolescence" at only eight months of age, so it's wise to learn what lies ahead before bringing a pup into the family.

BOXER TEMPERAMENT AND PERSONALITY

The versatility that makes the Boxer such an exceptional breed also indicates a number of temperament and personality traits that must be considered prior to becoming a Boxer owner. It's only fair to your family, your community, and your future Boxer that you learn as much as possible about the breed.

Loyalty

The Boxer's temperament is hard to fault. He always was and is a fiercely loyal family dog, bonding easily and permanently to his humans. Although his friendly nature extends to all people, he will nonetheless view strangers at the door warily and bark impressively.

His instinct for protection, not aggression, fosters this behavior and suits him as well to military and police work as to family life. Once a Boxer understands that guests welcomed into the home are no threat to his humans, he will show his enthusiasm with furious tail wagging and curl his body into the Boxer trademark "C" of wriggling joy.

Family Pet

The Boxer's natural fondness for children makes him a popular choice for a family pet. He seems to have the ability to discern older children who like an exuberant romp on the floor from younger children who

The Boxer is a fiercely loyal family dog who bonds easily and permanently to his humans.

topple over easily or aren't prepared for effusive Boxer attention. This is as much for the Boxer's safety as it is for the children's: Babies and toddlers might not be able to tell the difference between a gentle pat and a whack on the head. Ears, tails, and fur can be tempting baby pull toys, and even the most patient of dogs may react impulsively to the pain by snapping. Although any dog–child interaction should always be supervised, Boxer owners can be more confident than most about blending a dog into a child's family, or vice versa.

Boxers generally do well in multi-pet homes with other Boxers or dog breeds, especially if they've been together since puppyhood. Male–female pairings tend to develop most harmoniously. Two males can live happily together, especially if neutered, as can two females, but a struggle for dominance is always possible, and if one dog doesn't submit easily, there can be ongoing tension. If a Boxer dislikes another dog in the home, he can carry a lifetime grudge that may require permanent separation.

If your home includes other varieties of pets—cats, birds, rodents, etc.—you'll need to introduce them with care. Boxers are curious dogs, with a natural prey drive, so it's best to seek professional guidance before bringing a Boxer into your multi-pet home.

Intelligence and Trainability

The Boxer is highly intelligent, which accounts for his resourcefulness and trainability. He is not only quick to learn, he wants very much to please his human, and enjoys the interaction of training. Boxers quickly transition from obeying for treat rewards to making the conscious decision to obey and earn your praise. Trainability is not limited to obedience; the athletic Boxer succeeds at competitive sports like agility, flyball, and Schützhund.

Obedience Training

The Boxer isn't the tallest or heaviest breed, but he is one of the strongest. That lean, muscular build is not just attractive—it's powerful. Add momentum, and you have a dog whose enthusiastic welcome may knock over an unstable adult or a young child. A Boxer puppy gleefully jumping up on a visitor is darling; an adolescent or adult Boxer (weighing 50 pounds [22.5 kg] or more of muscle) jumping up is potentially dangerous. Good manners are a must for dogs, especially ultra-social Boxers. Obedience training can begin with puppy classes as soon as he's received all of his necessary shots.

Obedience training offers another benefit: mental stimulation. Boxers are easily bored, and bored dogs get into mischief that can turn destructive. In addition to acquiring good manners, obedience training provides the mental stimulation a Boxer needs to thrive.

PHYSICAL DESCRIPTION

The Boxer's physical appearance has undergone changes over the past century, and it continues to vary among countries

Boxer Prerequisites

Every dog breed presents its own set of challenges. The very qualities that make the Boxer such a fabulous companion can also manifest in less than adorable ways. There are varying degrees of unacceptable behavior, of course; chewing the table leg may not bother someone as much as sneaking onto the couch. It's therefore prudent to learn all you can about a Boxer's needs and habits to ensure that you can meet them before making a lifelong decision to add that special Boxer to your family.

(within the limits of the most current breed standard). German or American, brindle or fawn, natural ears or cropped, one thing remains constant: The Boxer's handsome elegance and dignified bearing render him a breed above breeds.

To fully appreciate the sum, you must understand the parts. What makes the ideal Boxer? The "breed standard" is a description of a breed's ideal physical and temperamental assets against which all dogs of that breed are measured. The first official Boxer breed standard, adopted by the AKC in 1904, was largely the same standard used in Germany at that time. Upon AKC-required establishment of individual breed clubs in the 1940s, the American Boxer Club (ABC) set the official Boxer standard and continues to oversee revisions. Breed standards written and revised by individual breed clubs must be approved by the AKC to become official. The authoritative Boxer standard has been revised nine times, most recently in 2005.

General Body Structure

The Boxer is a medium-sized, square-built, solid dog with a short back, strong limbs, and a short, close-fitting coat and well-formed muscles defined by taut skin. His proud carriage and sure movements denote energy; he exhibits a firm but flexible gait that covers substantial ground. He has a chiseled head that must be proportionate to body size, distinguished by a blunt muzzle that figures paramount when evaluating a puppy's head for potential conformation competition. Judges first evaluate overall balance and appearance, then pay special attention to the head.

The Boxer's coat is short, smooth, and close to the body, lending it a sleek appearance.

Size

Adult male Boxers measure 23 to 25 inches (58.5 to 63.5 cm) and weigh anywhere from 55 to 70 pounds (25 to 31.5 kg). Adult females measure 21.5 to 23.5 inches (54.5 to 60 cm) and weigh about 45 to 55 pounds (20.5 to 25 kg). How can you tell if your Boxer is at a healthy weight? Run your hands firmly but lightly down his rib cage. If your Boxer is overweight, you will have to press hard to feel the ribs. If he is underweight, the ribs will display too prominently.

Coat

The Boxer's coat is short, smooth, and close to the body, providing a sleek appearance.

Colors

According to the breed standard, only two colors are acceptable: fawn, which can range from a light tan to mahogany; and brindle, a pattern of black stripes on a fawn background. Areas of white—called "flash"—are acceptable, provided they do not exceed one third of the total color. A "flashy fawn" or "flashy brindle" Boxer will have an attractive contrast of white to his primary color. Even all-white Boxers are technically fawn colored—they have an excessive amount of white color to fawn. Similarly, "reverse" brindle or "black" brindle are really just brindle. They appear to have fawn stripes on a black background, but the size of the black stripes are disproportionately large compared to the fawn background.

Breeders consider all-white Boxers undesirable, not merely because they are nonstandard but because the gene mutation is often accompanied by deafness and/or other health problems. Consequently, white Boxers are regarded as a bloodline liability and are sometimes euthanized at birth. A better solution is to find responsible, loving homes for white Boxer puppies, predicated on the new owners' agreement never to breed these dogs.

A Boxer's eyes are typically dark brown and quite expressive.

Head and Neck

The Boxer's head is his hallmark, so it should display a proportionate muzzle-to-skull relationship. The short muzzle is one-third the length of the head and two-thirds the width of the skull. Unlike the taut skin elsewhere on the body, wrinkles typically appear on the forehead when the ears are erect, but they should not be deep, as with a Shar-Pei. The ubiquitous wrinkles on both sides of the muzzle are vestiges of the *Bullenbeissers'* deep folds that routed blood away from the dogs' nose and eyes during baiting and fighting.

The neck is round, of ample length, muscular, and clean, without dewlaps (pendulous folds). The elegant nape should blend smoothly into the withers (shoulders).

Eyes

One of the Boxer's most appealing traits is his unique expressiveness, and his eyes are especially so when combined with forehead wrinkling and head cocking. A Boxer's eyes are typically dark brown, although lighter shades sometimes appear in litters. A fawn Boxer with caramel-colored eyes is as striking, albeit nonstandard, as the preferred dark eyes on a "reverse" brindle

Boxer. A protective membrane (the *haws* or nictitating membrane, also known as the third eyelid) preferably has pigmented rims that are dark brown, but clear rims are acceptable, according to the breed standard. Unpigmented rims often reveal the tiny blood vessels in the eye and can make the eye appear inflamed even when nothing is wrong.

Ears

Boxer ears are at the center of international controversy. Strict proponents of the breed standard insist that cropped ears are an essential part of the Boxer's appearance; others maintain that the purpose behind cropped ears (to prevent bloody injuries during staged fights) is obsolete and therefore a purely cosmetic surgical and recuperative procedure that is unnecessarily stressful for puppies. Indeed, ear cropping is illegal in many countries, including Great Britain and Germany. Until recently, uncropped ears disqualified a Boxer for conformation competition in the United States; the breed standard was revised in 2005 to qualify natural-eared Boxers, specifying that ears "should be of moderate size, lying flat and close to the cheeks in repose but falling forward with a definite crease when alert."

In 2008, a two-year-old male, Bavaria's Heartbreaker, became the first natural-eared Boxer to win in an ABC specialty show.

PET SUITABILITY

Purebred dogs are usually classified as either "show quality" or "pet quality." The latter is a dog who does not sufficiently adhere to the official breed standard. In no way should this imply that a pet-quality Boxer is defective in health, overall appearance, or temperament. He may not be suitable to compete in the conformation show ring, but he will be a perfect pet to a loving family. Flawless health is never a guarantee, of course, but when you buy from a reputable breeder who has honestly evaluated her puppies for conformation, at least you're receiving more health history than if your pet Boxer came from a street-corner box marked "free puppies."

Climate

The Boxer's short, sleek coat is beautiful and low maintenance, but it offers little protection from the elements. You already know that a Boxer's love of humans precludes him from living full-time outside, but harsh winter weather and sultry summer days are tolerable only in short doses. Although his coat will thicken somewhat if he spends a good deal of time outdoors in chilly weather, it is insufficient insulation. The Boxer's brachycephalic (short-snouted) head makes him especially susceptible to hyperthermia (heatstroke), even when shade and water are provided. A good rule of thumb for discerning your Boxer's climate tolerance: If you have to don a coat to run outside and get the mail, it's too cold for your Boxer to be outside for an extended period. Similarly, if you step outside in summer and immediately start to perspire, imagine how much greater your discomfort if you were wearing a coat.

Speaking of hot temperatures, *never* leave your Boxer—or any other dog, for that matter—in a parked car. Even with the windows completely open, the interior heats up within minutes to an intolerable temperature, and your dog will suffer a miserable death. If you can't take him with you into air-conditioning, leave him at home.

Exercise Requirements

The Boxer is a working dog; not surprisingly, he is a highly energetic breed that requires routine, vigorous exercise. His physical and mental well-being rely on physical activity, and an exercised dog is more receptive to training sessions and less likely to be distracted. There's nothing a Boxer enjoys more than a good run at full tilt (in a safe, enclosed area, of course), and there's nothing more beautiful to watch than that sleek, muscular body streaking by with the grace and elegance of a puma. You'll need to ask yourself if your lifestyle can accommodate

The Boxer is a highly energetic breed that requires routine, vigorous exercise.

a commitment to working out with your Boxer and if you're willing to make that commitment.

Grooming Needs

One of the perks of Boxer ownership is the low-maintenance grooming they require. The Boxer's short, sleek fur requires only brief, regular brushing and a healthy diet rich in omega fatty acids to keep his skin supple and his coat shiny.

Boxers are naturally clean dogs who often groom themselves like cats. Bathing isn't really necessary unless they have rolled around in something nasty or are working as therapy dogs who may require a bath prior to therapeutic visits in hospitals and nursing homes. If you strongly favor a regular bathing schedule for your Boxer, keep them to a maximum of once monthly and use a gentle shampoo formulated especially for dogs. Shampoos for humans contain harsh detergents that can dry out a dog's skin and dull his coat, sometimes leading to uncomfortable itchiness and other skin problems.

Training Tidbit

Come is an easy "preschool" command you can teach your Boxer puppy from your first introduction. Kneel down some distance away and call for him in a happy voice. Greet him with as much enthusiasm as he displays in greeting you, and he'll quickly learn that obeying the *come* command results in positive attention.

Regular toenail trimming is part of any dog's grooming regimen, and you should accustom your puppy to having his paws and toes gently handled. Accidental injury while nail trimming is more likely if your Boxer is wriggling and pulling while you try to accurately position the clippers or filing tool. A relaxed dog makes this grooming task as simple as possible. (For more detailed grooming information, see Chapter 6: Boxer Grooming Needs.)

Health Issues

A healthy Boxer is the culmination of responsible breeding, a nutritionally balanced diet, plenty of exercise, and positive social interaction. All breeds have certain health issues to which they are predisposed, however. This does not imply that all dogs of a particular breed will develop these conditions, nor that they will not develop other conditions more prevalent in other breeds. It merely refers to physical conditions found more often in certain breeds than in others. It does not indicate a genetic weakness or particular frailty in any breed or dog. Boxer owners are wise to learn which ailments seem to manifest frequently in Boxers, including bloat, degenerative myelopathy (DM), cardiomyopathy, corneal ulcers, and hip dysplasia. (For more detailed information, see Chapter 8: Boxer Health and Wellness.)

Living Environment

The strong, active Boxer needs his space, so where you live is an important consideration when contemplating Boxer ownership.

Urban

If you're an urban dweller, you likely live in an apartment without a yard in which a large

The active Boxer needs space, so where you live is an important consideration.

dog can run nor a living room large enough for high-speed laps around the sectional sofa. Most cities do have dog parks, but Boxers are often unpredictable when interacting with other, unfamiliar dogs. You will need to find a suitable place to take the city-dwelling Boxer every day to stretch his legs and enjoy the outdoors, weather permitting. Many urbanites hire professional dog walkers, but not all walks are created equal; you'll want to arrange for exercise appropriate for a Boxer, not a Chihuahua.

Suburban

Suburban dwellers have more to offer Boxers in the way of space, indoors and out. Even if the suburban home lacks a fenced-in yard, usually enough area is available to erect a dog run or mini-kennel. "Invisible" fences—an

area marked by an electric barrier that works in concert with a special radio receiver collar worn by the dog—are very popular with many suburban residents but have definite drawbacks. They are not infallible; most dogs will brave a momentary electric shock if strongly tempted by something beyond the designated perimeter. A strong adrenalin rush can easily overcome temporary pain. Nor will invisible fences prevent other animals from entering your yard. Above all, remember that the Boxer should never be considered an "outside" dog. Not only would he keenly feel the lack of human companionship, he cannot tolerate temperature extremes.

Rural

Rural living is well suited to a Boxer, who loves to run and explore the great outdoors. No matter how isolated your home is, though, precautions must be taken to maintain your dog's safety. Even vast acreage ends somewhere, and proper containment ensures that your Boxer won't make his way into vehicular traffic or another property with unfamiliar animals or intolerant humans. A rural environment also warrants extra vigilance in protection against parasites and hazardous vegetation.

Sociability

Boxers adore their humans, so be prepared to give of yourself fully if you add one to your family. As pack animals, dogs are instinctively social, and Boxers are especially needy of human companionship. They are content just to be in the same room with you, but they prefer to be sprawled out on your lap or curled up right next to you. Boxers provide a special affection that is unlike that of any other breed, but they require it as well. If you're not the demonstrative type, you may fare better with a more independent, less emotionally engaged breed. But if you like the idea of giving yourself body and soul to a dog who will return a hundredfold the love

Multi-Dog Tip

A puppy who joins a multi-dog family will learn many of the "rules" from the established dogs, such as where to eliminate and which food and toys the dogs are willing to share. Continue to supervise your new puppy's interaction with established dogs until you're sure of family harmony.

Want to Know More?

For more information on how to teach the *sit–stay*, see Chapter 9: Boxer Training.

he receives, there is no better choice than the Boxer.

With Children

Boxers are particularly wonderful with children. They are always ready to play, and a romp of safe, playful roughhousing with older children on the floor or in the yard is a good source of physical and social stimulation. They are very protective of children and have been known to lie underneath a baby's crib during naptime. However, they may not understand that a toddler just learning to walk is easily toppled by an enthusiastic Boxer greeting. As with any family dog, interaction with children should be supervised at all times. This is as much for the dog's protection as the children's. A toddler's idea of a gentle pat may manifest as a hearty thwack. Supervised interaction is the perfect opportunity to educate children on the do's and don'ts of doggy interaction:

- Never run up to or chase an unfamiliar dog, who may feel threatened and bite.

- Never take a toy or food away from a dog while he is busy with it.

- Never sneak up on a dog.

- Never startle a sleeping dog.

- When meeting a new dog, ask his owner if you may pet him. If consent is given, gently hold out the back of your closed fist for him to sniff, which is less threatening than an open hand or fingers thrust in the dog's face.

Many Boxers can live together in harmony, although this depends on a variety of factors, including age and gender.

In your search for the right family pet, visit several breeders and meet their Boxers. Take the whole family (who will be living under the same roof with the dog), and observe their reactions to different Boxers. Everyone loves a puppy, but would your youngsters find intimidating the sight of a 60-pound (27-kg) male Boxer with cropped ears? The breed's natural exuberance can be scary for young children, and the last thing you should do is to bring a Boxer home if any family member is hesitant or uncomfortable with the idea. Make sure that everyone's aware that the cute, cuddly three-month-old pup will one day be a large, strong, adult Boxer. It's important to educate children on the difference between mouthing, or play biting, and a serious bite inflicted in fear, pain, defense, or aggression. Puppies will play bite anything they can get their mouths on, including human body parts. Their teeth are needle sharp, and children need to learn how to avoid puppy bites, just as puppies need to learn that all mouthing isn't acceptable. Their mother will chastise them if they bite too hard, and their littermates will likewise communicate if a play bite is too rough or unwelcome. Part of a dog's all-important socialization can begin with curtailing puppy mouthing, and kids can participate in this ongoing process.

Boxers are always ready to play.

With Strangers

Successful socialization means presenting your Boxer to people of different genders, ages, ethnicities, and physical characteristics. Boxers love people in general but are very protective of their human family. It's important for your Boxer to learn that not all strangers are threatening. Conversely, if your Boxer understands that some strangers are *not* always welcome into the home, his protective instincts will provide the best security system you could have, free of charge.

Your Boxer will pick up cues from you, the pack leader, while you're out and about. If someone approaches and you hang back warily, he will detect your hesitancy. He may seek to protect you by barking at the stranger or assuming a "tread carefully"

stance with the fur on his back standing up. If, however, a stranger approaches you and you maintain a relaxed demeanor with your dog short-leashed at your side, he will presume that you are comfortable with the situation, and he can get acquainted.

With Other Dogs

Same-sex pairings can work, provided that dominance is established and accepted. If the dogs are constantly challenging each other for the alpha position, harmony is unlikely. Behaviorists recommend introducing an established dog to a new pack member with both dogs on leash and treats on hand to reward relaxed, appropriate behavior. The new dog should remain in a *sit-stay* position, or at least standing still, while you permit the resident dog to calmly approach the stationary newcomer. Keep the atmosphere happy and lighthearted, with plenty of treats to reward them for not snapping or growling. Once the established dog has had a chance to investigate the new pack mate, switch places and let the new dog repeat the exercise. If all continues well, allow them both to investigate each other, still on leash. Most likely, they will both be excited to have a new playmate, and the relationship will emerge harmonious.Until pack position is clearly understood, the established dog may vocally warn his new "sibling" if the latter gets too close to his food or favorite toy. Alternatively, the new dog may challenge the resident's alpha position. This situation will resolve itself in one of three ways:

1. The established dog will retain dominance.
2. The new dog will acquire alpha status.
3. The two dogs will compete for alpha status but neither dog will acquiesce. This conflict can ultimately require permanent separation of the dogs.

With Other Pets

If you have other pets in the home, it's important to realize that not all Boxers enjoy sharing their humans. The breed's ancient warring heritage means that some animal aggression *may* linger in the genes. Protocol must be followed to properly introduce a new Boxer to your other pets or your established Boxer to a new pet. If the other pets are small prey animals like rabbits or guinea pigs, keep them in a cage and allow your Boxer to sniff them through the enclosure.

If you already own a cat, you have a better chance for successful integration with a puppy who can grow up with the cat as a pack member. If your cat is declawed, elderly, or a kitten, he can be injured by a dog with a strong prey drive or one that is prone to rough play. Ideally, introduce the potential packmates before you take possession of the newcomer. This will spare you the stress and heartache of having to rehome one of your pets because of discord.

CHAPTER 2

FINDING AND PREPPING FOR YOUR BOXER PUPPY

Puppies require much of the same commitment as human babies, and for a while your world will revolve around your puppy's well-being and adjustment, a temporarily high-maintenance phase that is well balanced by the many gifts a family pet brings.

WHY A PUPPY MAY BE RIGHT FOR YOU

Just as you wouldn't bring home a human baby without adequate preparation, much needs to be decided and accomplished before bringing home your Boxer baby. You must be mentally and practically ready to cope with housetraining, teething, puppy-proofing your living space, and the pup's transition from communal litter to independence.

A puppy is a clean slate, without previous ownership and bad habits to unlearn. You can enjoy watching him grow and discover the world, often alongside your human children. You can initiate him into family activities or help him discover new ones. He will bond with you as his pack leader and parent figure, and you can take pride in the task you've undertaken for his entire well-being. The love and loyalty you'll receive in return is priceless.

WHERE TO FIND THE PUPPY OF YOUR DREAMS

Available puppies are advertised in newspapers and on bulletin boards, the Internet, and street corners. But the best resource for a Boxer puppy is a reputable breeder who knows the dog's heritage and has tested him for health and temperament issues within the breed.

Breeders

Responsible breeders are often avid dog show participants. But even the fortunate breeder with abundant acreage and living space has a limit to how many dogs she can responsibly care for. Puppies who do not closely adhere to the breed standard and are not good candidates for conformation competition make wonderful pets. They are usually less expensive than their show-quality littermates, too.

Locating a good breeder is no different than finding any other type of trustworthy professional. You want someone with experience, integrity, and compatibility with your needs. Because word of mouth is usually the best resource for such a professional, ask other Boxer owners where they obtained their

The best resource for a Boxer puppy is a reputable breeder who knows his heritage and has tested him for health and temperament issues.

they may be able to refer you to one in your area. Remember that most breeders listed in magazines have paid for the advertisement; the magazine is not necessarily endorsing them. While these breeders are theoretically more professional and knowledgeable about Boxers than breeders with local newspaper ads touting "Boxer puppies for sale," you should do some research. How long has the kennel been around? How did the breeder become interested in Boxers? Can she provide documentation of health and temperament testing of her puppies? Does she request that you relinquish custody of the Boxer to her if, at any time during the dog's life, you can no longer care for him? If possible, visit any breeder you are considering to see for yourself how the dogs and kennel are maintained.

dogs. Ask veterinarians in your area if they know any Boxer breeders. Tell all of your friends and acquaintances, even those who don't own dogs or are not familiar with Boxers, that you're looking for a reputable breeder. Exponential promulgation is the key to successful networking.

You can also find responsible breeders through organizations and publications. National dog magazines often have comprehensive indices of breeders located throughout the United States. Even if the Boxer breeders listed are not located nearby,

Another convenient resource is the American Boxer Club (ABC). Their website can direct you to the Boxer club of your state or region, which can then recommend some breeders to you. Dog culture, especially within specific breeds, is communal. Respected breeders receive referrals.

Advice on finding a good breeder is incomplete without addressing which resources to avoid. Some can be well intentioned but undereducated, while some can be downright unethical or illegal. The chances of obtaining a healthy, even-tempered, carefully bred Boxer puppy for an appropriate price can be dubious via these avenues:

- **Puppy mills**: Puppy mills are abusive, immoral dog breeding operations that care nothing for proper breeding nor the well-being of their brood dogs. Their sole concern is to profit from breeding and selling as many puppies as possible as quickly as possible. The source for your Boxer puppy should be fastidious about breeding conditions and the standards of their puppies.

- **Newspaper or bulletin board ads**: "Boxer puppies for sale" can represent undesirable scenarios: an irresponsible pet owner whose dog mated randomly, a backyard breeder for whom Boxer breeding is a casual hobby, or even an abandoned litter whose parentage is in question. Price tags on these puppies may compare with those of serious breeders, but most likely aren't justified by the health and temperament benefits of careful, deliberate breeding.

- **Internet**: The Internet is rife with unscrupulous breeders and scams surrounding dogs. They take advantage of naive dog lovers by providing false information, reneging on health guarantees and promises of fee reimbursements, willfully selling sick puppies, or simply asking for full payment in advance for shipping of nonexistent puppies. While some Internet breeder ads and websites are obviously legitimate, sight-unseen transactions are not the best way to add a Boxer to your family. You have no way of knowing the true conditions of a breeding kennel or the ethics of an unfamiliar breeder unless you see for yourself.

By the Numbers

Puppies should remain with their mother and littermates for at least eight weeks in order to learn appropriate pack behavior before going to their new homes.

Not even the best reputed, experienced breeder can guarantee a puppy who will be free of illness throughout his lifetime. Like humans, dogs are living longer due to advances in medical science. The longer the life, the greater the chance of developing some type of illness. But the odds are improved considerably by starting with a breeder whose primary concern is betterment of the breed.

Paperwork

All important milestones in our lives involve documentation—birth certificates, diplomas, marriage licenses—and obtaining a well-bred Boxer puppy carries its own paperwork too. A conscientious breeder will have a packet of information for you to take home with your puppy. It will include a sales receipt, basic statistics on the pup (birth date, sex, color, etc.), medical history (first shots, worming), certificates of registration and health, family tree, feeding instructions (including the kind of food the puppy's been fed since weaning), and any other pertinent information, such as veterinary referrals, books on training, and recommended toys.

Shelters and Rescues

Animal shelters and rescues occasionally have purebred puppies available for adoption,

Puppies are like human babies in that they must eat and sleep frequently to thrive.

but health and breeding information may be sketchy. If you adopt a Boxer or Boxer-mix puppy from a shelter or rescue, understand that you may confront health or temperament issues from a mysterious past.

Conversely, adopting a homeless or special-needs Boxer is a compassionate act that can save the life of a shelter dog who may face euthanasia if not adopted or a rescued dog whose foster home is only temporary. Adopted and rescued dogs are grateful for their second chance in life and repay the kindness with

Want to Know More?

For more information on how to housetrain a puppy, see Chapter 4: Training Your Puppy.

unswerving loyalty and affection. If you're prepared to offer a forever home to a needy dog, come what may, adoption is a loving choice you will never regret.

Paperwork

The paperwork involved in a shelter/rescue adoption differs from breeder paperwork in subject matter but not volume! Paperwork equals information that will enable you to provide the best care possible to your adopted dog. Shelters/rescue organizations will provide you with the dog's medical records and any personal history they have on the dog, such as how he came to be in the shelter, the previous owner's lifestyle and circumstances, and any favorite toys or treats. If the dog was a stray, the shelter may not have any facts but will estimate the dog's age and evaluate his temperament and physical condition.

Most shelters and rescue organizations require a completed application form to begin the adoption process. Once you are approved for adoption and are ready to bring home your new dog, you will probably be required to sign an adoption agreement containing specific information such as an indemnity clause, dog return agreement, and guarantee of lifetime ownership, veterinary care, and nurturing home care.

BEFORE YOUR PUPPY COMES HOME

As imprudent as it would be to bring a human baby from the hospital to a home without diapers, a crib, and nursing supplies, your home should be prepared and stocked with the supplies necessary for your new puppy's well-being.

Puppy-Proof Your Home

Before you bring home your new Boxer, you'll need to make sure that his environment is as safe and comfortable as possible. Even though he won't be left unsupervised or uncrated in your home, hazards must be removed. Puppies will teethe on anything they can find, and you don't want him munching on a nice, chewy electric cord or an intriguing kitchen cleaner spray bottle.

Walk through every area that will be accessible to your Boxer puppy: house, garage,

When uncrated, your Boxer will enjoy a cozy bed where he can relax at will.

Training Tidbit

and yard. Potential dangers often lurk in the most unlikely places: toxic plants, upper-story railings spaced widely enough to catch a puppy's head or allow him to fall through, unsupervised garage access where a puppy might find toxic fluids or sharp tools, shelving with heavy objects that can fall over or be pulled off by an inquisitive pup, swimming pools, hot tubs, wading pools, ponds. Even small, everyday items like thumbtacks, matches, keys, writing instruments, razors, chocolate, liquor, pesticides, and cleaners recently applied in the house can sicken or otherwise harm a young puppy. Also supervise him around steep stairs and tall furniture that can cause falls. Try to look around your home through a curious puppy's eyes to see what he might decide to investigate.

Set Up a Schedule

Puppies are like human babies in that they must eat and sleep frequently to thrive. They will eat three to four small meals, evenly spaced throughout the day, from the time they are weaned until they are approximately six months old. As your puppy grows, you can reduce the frequency of meals to twice daily. A feeding schedule is important for two reasons. To develop good eating habits, puppies should learn that they have a certain timeframe in which to eat the apportioned food provided to them at mealtimes. "Free feeding"—having unlimited food available at all times—enables overeating and competition for food with other pets. A meal schedule is also important for successful housetraining. Half the battle of housetraining is anticipating quickly enough the pup's need to eliminate and removing him to the designated spot in time. You can almost always encourage a young puppy to eliminate after meals, reinforcing the message of eliminating in a specific area. Similarly, pups should also be taken to their elimination area immediately upon awaking in the morning or from a nap, before they have a chance to walk around indoors.

A puppy's schedule requires adherence if you hope to quickly train him where he should eliminate. His immature bladder requires voiding every few hours, so nighttime elimination trips will accelerate housetraining. It means disrupted sleep for you, but a puppy who is taken to the same elimination spot regularly throughout the day *and* night will more quickly understand your intentions than a puppy who is taken outside to eliminate during the day but left in his crate to eliminate indoors in the middle of the night.

Structure provides puppies with a sense of security, just as it does for human children. It will take time for a puppy to adjust to your household schedule, but starting him off with a schedule of his own facilitates this adjustment phase.

Purchase Supplies

"Be prepared" is a good motto for new puppy owners, and there are certain essentials you'll want to purchase before bringing your Boxer pup home.

Bed

When uncrated, your Boxer will enjoy a cozy bed of his own where he can relax at will. You can fashion a bed with just an old blanket or two (a Boxer likes nothing more than to paw up the bedding you have carefully arranged into a disorganized mound and plop down onto it), or buy one of the many varieties of beds available in stores. Some are filled with cedar shavings to discourage odors and bugs; some are filled with a spongy foam material and have a removable, washable cover of fleece and/ or fabric. You can even find dog beds filled with down or pricey memory foam. A bolster around the top of the bed provides a sense of security that appeals to a dog's denning instincts. If your dog's crate is located where he can see the family, you may wish to appoint it with comfortable bedding he will use for naps and relaxation even while supervised. Whatever type of bed you choose, keep it clean, comfortable, and appropriately sized for many years of enjoyment.

Bowls

Food and water dishes are commonly made of plastic, stainless steel, or ceramic. Pet dishes made from any other material should be discussed with your vet, to ensure that nothing in the material will cause adverse chemical reactions to the ingredients in your puppy's food and make him sick. Even the plastic in feeding bowls can cause an allergic skin reaction around the mouth. Ceramics are easily broken if dropped, but stainless steel is durable, sanitary, and easy to clean.

Collar

You'll want to start acclimating your new Boxer to wearing a collar before you begin leash walking and obedience training. Collars come in many materials: metal links, nylon mesh, leather, and even plastic. Metal link collars are used for obedience training only; they're hazardous for everyday wear. The links can too easily snag on branches, fences, or other objects and accidentally strangle the dog. The best collar for your puppy is sturdy, adjustable in size, and snaps together with a flat buckle. An appropriately sized collar will not be so loose that the dog can wriggle his head out of it, nor so tight that you cannot easily insert a finger in between the collar and the dog's neck. A comfortable fit is secure, with no impediment to breathing and swallowing.

For walking, many dog owners prefer to use a harness, which fits around the dog's body and avoids leash pulling at the neck. Head halters are also popular alternatives to collars for walking a dog without pulling. But

A conventional leash made of leather or strong nylon works best for walks.

remember that the neck collar affords you a means of control when the dog is wearing it, something to grab if he needs to be restrained. Talk to your breeder or veterinarian about the best collar choice for your Boxer puppy.

Clothes

Unless you live in a harsh northern climate, your Boxer's coat will keep him comfortable outdoors in most temperatures. But his short fur will not offer much protection if he must be outside in rain, snow, or ice. Dog parkas and raincoats will keep him warm and dry, and waterproof boots will keep his paws dry and protected from ice shards and salt or chemical ice-melting pellets. In general, if your Boxer gets wet, rub him dry with a towel and make sure that his environment is warm and free of drafts.

Crate

Dogs are den animals who feel secure in a protected or sheltered area. An appropriately sized crate provides a safe haven for your Boxer and peace of mind for you. After a brief adjustment period, a properly trained pup enjoys having a special place of his own where he can spend time even when the family is around. When a puppy must be left unsupervised for any length of time, crating is a must. Not only does it ensure his safety, but it is a useful housetraining tool, as dogs instinctively avoid soiling their beds.

Crates are usually constructed of heavy wire or sturdy opaque plastic. It's a matter of preference which one you choose. Some dog owners claim that the opaque crate more closely mimics a den and offers a greater sense of shelter. Others say that their dogs prefer wire crates because they can see what's going on around them. Proper crate location is essential too: Select a warm place where your puppy can rest, away from foot traffic but still within sight of the family.

The crate should *never* be used as a prison or a place of punishment. It should be a cozy nook that your Boxer pup will enjoy. It will keep your puppy safe when you can't supervise him, and it will foster independence.

Grooming Supplies

You won't need many grooming supplies for the low-maintenance Boxer, but basics include a soft bristle brush for weekly touch-ups; a shedding comb for semi-annual coat "blow outs," when fur thickens and sheds copiously with seasonal changes; a mild dog shampoo; and nail trimming tool. A puppy's small nails are easily trimmed with a pair of clippers, or you can utilize a battery-powered, hand-held grinding tool that files down the nail and smoothes rough edges. You'll be performing regular nail care throughout your Boxer's life, so it's important to acquaint him with the procedure early and carefully. If he learns to fear nail trimming, you will fight a lifelong battle that's unpleasant for both of you. Ask your breeder or veterinarian for the proper way to accustom your puppy to safe nail trimming.

Identification

Even the most vigilant of humans may one day be faced with a missing pet, and the last thing you want under such circumstances is an unidentifiable dog. Fortunately, several identification options are available to ensure that this never happens to you and your Boxer.

Tags: ID tags aren't infallible means of identifying your dog. They can fall off, be removed by someone, or contain outdated information. Yet they are still an inexpensive, simple way to provide basic identification on a collar that your dog wears anyway. ID tags should have you or your vet's name and phone number. Alternatively, you can order a collar with this information stitched into the fabric, which removes the possibility of lost tags. When your puppy receives his first rabies shot, which is required by law, the vet will provide a certification tag to be affixed to the collar with any ID tags. Should your dog be at large, a current rabies tag will inform strangers that he's been vaccinated. A stray dog without a rabies tag who bites someone risks euthanasia because the diagnostic test for canine rabies is performed posthumously.

Microchipping and Tattooing: More permanent and reliable than removable tags and collars, tattooing involves a registration number painlessly (the needle doesn't need to be as deeply inserted into the epidermis as with human tattoos) inscribed on the inner thigh, where fur is sparse and the number most visible. The number corresponds to owner information on file with a registry that will notify the owner that someone has recovered the dog. However, it may be challenging to keep the dog calm with the loud noise of the instrument, as well as immobile during the process. Free touch-ups may be required in the future because the ink may blur over time.

Microchipping is similar in that each chip's serial number is entered into a national registry of owner information. The computer microchip, about the size of a grain of rice and containing owner information, is painlessly inserted under the dog's skin. Most veterinarians and animal control offices have the scanning device that detects a microchip's number, which is then called into the registry, which notifies the owner. Microchipping is generally preferred over tattooing because it lasts a lifetime and is more quickly and easily applied.

Leash (or Lead)

One trip to your local pet supply store and you'll see that leashes come in several varieties. Retractable nylon cord leashes of lengths up to 16 feet (5 m) are convenient on walks because they allow the frisky Boxer to pick up his pace without forcing you into a run. However, the longer the leash is extended, the less control you have over your pup— not an ideal situation when he's just learning to walk on a leash and obey you. Moreover, an adult Boxer is very strong and can snap a retractable lead. When you begin obedience training, you'll want to use a leash that's 6 feet (2 m) long that helps teach the basic commands.

Standard-length leashes made of durable metal links are sturdy but can weigh heavily on the dog's neck when attached to his collar, especially if he's a young puppy. This will not make walks pleasant for him and will undermine your leash training. A conventional leash made of leather or strong nylon works best for walks.

Toys

Toys are more than playthings for puppies; they stimulate mental growth and support physical dexterity. They are props for playtime with your Boxer as you build your relationship, and they are comforting reminders of home when your puppy can't be with you.

Chew toys like Nylabones are probably the most useful playthings you will buy for your Boxer. Dogs have an instinctive need to chew. It cleans their teeth and gums and

Dual-Purpose Toys

Dog toys nowadays have more of a purpose than they used to. The good old tennis ball and knotted rope will always be fun standbys, but people realize that if a dog's mind is occupied, he won't become bored and search for mischief. Treat-dispensing balls and other geometric shapes motivate a dog to figure out how to get a favorite snack to get the treat inside. Balls equipped with motion-activated recordings of your voice can help calm a nervous dog. A rubber toy filled with peanut butter, cheese, or other tasty treat in the middle will usually keep a dog busy for as long as a drop of filling remains.

helps keep incisors sharp. Teething puppies of four to eight months of age especially need to chew as they lose their puppy or "milk" teeth and adult teeth grow in. The best and safest chew toys do not have parts that can cause choking or illness if swallowed. Rubber squeaky toys are very popular with puppies, but you must supervise play at all times. The rubber can be flimsy, and nothing is as fun for a puppy as tearing apart a rubber toy to get at the squeaker, which poses a choking hazard. Sturdy, heavy-duty rubber toys can stand up to the most enthusiastic chewer and won't shred. Another popular dog chew toy is rawhide, which comes in shapes like shoes or bones with knots at each end. Dogs adore this chewy, tasty, dried toy, but cowhide is indigestible and can cause intestinal blockage. A cow marrow or knuckle bone is a better choice, as long as you take care to replace it if it starts to splinter.

A puppy will be ready to leave his mother and littermates at around eight weeks of age.

Whatever toys you choose, make sure they're safe and size appropriate. Rotate your puppy's access to them so he does not grow bored. Toys will give you hours of entertainment too, as you watch your Boxer play.

BRINGING YOUR BOXER PUPPY HOME

You are about to bring home your new Boxer puppy, and life will never be the same. That's a *good* thing. This adorable bundle of joy is completely dependent on you for his very existence, and you have a hard act to follow: mom.

Ready or Not?

Puppies are typically ready to leave their mother and littermates at eight weeks, but they will still miss the security, companionship, and love of their first home. Joining your family will take adjustment on everyone's part, and it helps to understand what lies ahead during those first few weeks.

Your puppy should be weaned, wormed, and up to date on vaccinations before you arrive at the breeder's to take him home. He should look and behave as healthy and happy as the day you selected him, with a shiny coat, free of parasites, and eyes bright with energy. Still, your first order of business will be to have him examined by your veterinarian within three days of taking him home. If you can make an appointment in advance to correspond with the time you will be collecting your puppy from his breeder, so much the better. Not only is it a good opportunity for vet and puppy to meet each other and bond a little, but it's imperative for the Boxer's health and well-being that any underlying problems be identified. The sooner you discover a problem, the easier it will be to discern its origin.

The First Day

You'll begin housetraining your puppy as soon as you bring him home. Before he comes home with you for the first time, ask his breeder if you can put in a plastic bag some dirt, mulch, or shavings where the puppies have urinated. First thing when you arrive home with your Boxer pup, immediately bring him out to the spot where you've sprinkled the scented shavings or mulch on the ground. He will identify the urine scent and eliminate there, inferring that it's an acceptable elimination place. There will be mistakes ahead, but every little thing you can do to ensure his success helps.

Show your new Boxer his bed or crate where he can take a nap after all the excitement of arriving home. Puppies play hard and sleep hard, so be sure to give him a chance to rest in between cuddles and play sessions. Remember to take him outside to eliminate immediately after sleeping, eating, and drinking.

The First Night

To make your puppy's separation from his mother and littermates easier, provide him with something that smells familiar. A puppy's sense of smell is very strong, and certain scents will be very comforting to him. Take a baby blanket, soft puppy toy, or towel to the breeder's a few days in advance and ask her to "scent" the item for you. She'll have the mother lie on it for a day or two to embed her scent onto it. When you take it home and give it your puppy, his mother's scent will do much to comfort him in this strange new place. Chances are you will all get a better night's sleep.

Another trick for comforting your puppy during his first crucial nights in your home is to wrap a ticking clock in a soft cloth or a pair of socks and place it in his crate with him. The ticking is thought to comfort the puppy by mimicking his mother's heartbeat. Likewise, it's thought that a hot water bottle

Your puppy should be weaned, wormed, and up to date on vaccinations before you take him home.

wrapped in a soft blanket simulates the warm pile of puppies on which he slept at the breeder. You might also try leaving on a radio or television with soft, soothing music or voices to keep him company. You can even buy music CDs with instruments and lyrics designed to be soothing to dogs, the result of extensive research on what types of sounds appeal to them.

If it takes your puppy a while to become accustomed to sleeping in his crate alone, be patient. After all, he's starting a new life, and it's a tremendous adjustment. Do all that you can to make him feel safe and comfortable.

The typical eight-week-old puppy's bladder is too immature to endure the entire night without voiding. Like a human baby, he will wake every few hours during the night and probably cry. This is a good chance to continue the housetraining you began as soon as you brought him home. Remove him from his crate immediately to the outdoor elimination area you've designated. When he voids, praise him with as much enthusiasm as you can muster in the middle of the night.

The First Few Weeks

Your life may seem a little out of order in the weeks following your puppy's homecoming, but it's all for a worthy cause: the happy assimilation of your new Boxer. Amid the chaos, a more predictable routine will emerge. Your pup will get his bearings and start adjusting to the family's schedule. This is a crucial time in his development and for the socialization that's such an integral part. It's never too soon to start teaching good manners and habits. Behaviors that you find cute in your puppy may not be acceptable when he's an adult. Educating yourself on puppy behavior and registering for puppy kindergarten is in everyone's best interest, especially your Boxer.

Multi-Dog Tip

If you are adding more than one Boxer puppy to your family—perhaps a couple of littermates—thinking that they will be inseparable playmates and friends, remember how much Boxers love their humans! Both puppies will probably prefer your company over each other's.

Above all, enjoy puppyhood to the fullest. Before you know it, that small bundle of love will have become a solid, lightning-quick locomotive of energy. When it's three in the morning and you're shivering in the frosty air, praising your puppy for piddling in the right place, every lick of that little pink tongue will make it all worthwhile.

CHAPTER 3

CARE OF YOUR BOXER PUPPY

A Boxer puppy can melt your heart like no other breed. His baby fur is just a touch more velvety, his wee pink toe pads a bit more tender. That round puppy belly seems warmer, his puppy breath slightly sweeter.

These delights are not free of charge, though, unless you happen to have a Boxer-breeding friend who is willing to let you reap the playtime pleasures of puppyhood without its long-term responsibilities. But if you've researched the breed, located a reputable breeder, and prepared yourself emotionally, financially, and physically to welcome a Boxer into your life, you'll be taking on one of the most rewarding responsibilities you'll ever have.

FEEDING A PUPPY

Nursing puppies receive all their required nutrition and antibodies from their mother's milk, but once they're weaned, it's up to their humans to provide the right food on which a puppy will thrive.

Puppies need frequent, small meals of a high-quality food and fresh water available at all times. Your puppy will have been eating solid food for about four to six weeks before you bring him home, so ask the breeder what food she's been feeding the litter and lay in a supply of the same food. If you prefer a different kind that's equally nutritious, you can eventually integrate it into your puppy's diet. At first, however, it's best to continue feeding the puppy the food he's been eating, as his immature stomach isn't equipped to handle abrupt dietary changes.

Pups expend a lot of energy during their formative months and need to be "refueled" appropriately.

Feeding Schedules

A puppy's general feeding schedule is four times a day until the dog is eight to ten weeks old, spaced evenly throughout the day, until he's about two years old. Then they should be fed three times a day until they are four to five months of age and then two times a day for the rest of their lives. Dogs mature at varying rates; feeding schedules can and should be adjusted accordingly.

In the Unites States, where food is abundant, we tend to overindulge ourselves. We should not make this mistake with our dogs. For many people, food equals love, but a more sensible demonstration of love for our dogs is to feed them what they need, not necessarily what they—or we—want. Your breeder or veterinarian can guide you on how much to feed your puppy at each meal. By providing a constant supply of the proper amount of "fuel," your puppy's body will utilize it optimally.

Commercial dog food packages usually provide feeding guidelines based on the age and weight of your puppy. However, if he seems insatiable and your vet approves, supplement the portions of his food with a little cooked brown rice or whole-grain, low-sugar cereal. The bulk will keep him satisfied longer without adding a lot of extra calories.

Treats will be an important component in your puppy's diet, especially when you begin

Puppies need small, high-quality meals in order to thrive.

training, so it's important to buy or make wholesome treats that complement his diet and don't upset his stomach. The appeal of treats to a dog is good taste, but many commercial dog treats use unhealthy fats and artificial ingredients to achieve that taste. Table scraps are never an appropriate part of a balanced canine diet, so they shouldn't be considered a treat source. Wholesome commercial dog treats or treats you make yourself (an Internet search turns up many easy recipes) are the best choice for your little Boxer.

There are basically two ways to feed a dog: scheduled feeding and free-feeding. As the name implies, free-feeding means providing unlimited food all the time. Scheduled feeding is, obviously, on a schedule. Common sense dictates that apportioned food at specific intervals is the healthy way to feed a dog, yet some dog food companies advocate free-feeding. To make an educational choice, let's understand the options and their repercussions.

By the Numbers

Puppies are weaned at approximately four weeks of age, when the mother makes herself less and less available for nursing. Breeders will then supplement with nutritionally appropriate solid food. In the wild, bitches supplement the weaning pups' diet by regurgitating partially digested food. Puppies will lick their mother's mouth to encourage her to regurgitate.

Scheduled Feeding

Puppies will eat about four small meals throughout the day, in between naps and playtimes. The amount will vary with each dog, but generally a puppy should have about 1/4 cup of food at a time. As a puppy grows, meals will become less frequent and appropriately increase in amount. For guidance, consult your vet or breeder.

If your lifestyle keeps you away from home much of the day, arrange for someone to come in a few times to feed the puppy and take him outside. His frequent-meal schedule will last several months, and you'll need to accommodate it.

To keep scheduled feeding scheduled, limit the time that meals are available to the puppy. To discourage picky eating, pick up his food dish after ten minutes, even if he hasn't eaten it all. He will learn quickly that his window of opportunity is limited, and he needs to adapt to it or bide his time until the next meal.

Scheduled feeding encourages regular elimination, which in turn aids your housetraining efforts. If you take your puppy outside after every meal, he will most likely eliminate, reinforcing the message.

Free-Feeding

Anyone who has ever taken a cruise vacation will understand the problem with free-feeding: an endless buffet served around the clock, every day of the week. Most dogs won't stop eating when they are sated. Just as humans tend to do, dogs keep eating because it tastes good. Some dogs, especially rescued dogs, may harbor an instinct that tells them to eat all that they can while it's available. A free-feeding Boxer will probably become overweight, lethargic, and less enthusiastic about food. Obedience training may become difficult because he won't be motivated by treats.

Dogs in the wild experience long interludes between meals. Their digestive systems aren't designed to accommodate continuous, unlimited eating. They rest after digestion and prepare for the next meal.

Free-feeding can also promote begging, a bad habit you don't want your Boxer puppy to learn. If his food is available at all times, he will become pretty bored by it. Your meatloaf will smell a lot more enticing than the same

Scheduled feeding involves limiting the time that meals are available to the puppy.

tired kibble in his bowl. He may start to ignore his food completely and wait for table scraps. This is not only bad manners but unhealthy, because the foundation of any healthy, happy dog is built on proper nutrition.

Understanding Food Package Labels

Health-conscious humans have learned that closely reading the ingredient lists on commercially produced food packages can confirm, contradict, or elucidate the nutrition information promulgated in media advertising and on label faces. A product advertised as low fat may have extra sugar added to compensate in taste. Something touted as sugar free may have a very high carbohydrate and/or added fat content. We have to examine the nutritional content breakdown on the label to know exactly what we're getting—a confusing task that's even harder when it comes to dog food labels.

If a dog food label declares the contents "100% nutritionally complete," it's appropriate for all life stages. On the other hand, if the label specifies a certain phase, such as "puppies" or "seniors," the food is formulated especially to meet the nutritional needs of that phase. Dry puppy kibble may be of a finer texture that's easier on a puppy's immature digestive tracts than adult kibble.

Puppies and Protein

Controversy over the appropriate amount of protein in puppy-formula commercial dog foods may warrant consultation with your breeder and veterinarian. It's been said that the higher amount of protein in puppy food (compared to that of adult-formula food) fosters an accelerated growth rate. The puppy's bone development cannot keep pace with the rest of the body, potentially causing hip and/or other joint problems later in life. This is thought to be of particular concern in large and giant breeds, so Boxer owners should seek professional advice on this subject to ensure that they provide the best diet possible for their puppies.

Ingredients

Ingredients are listed on labels in descending order of amount. The first few ingredients listed comprise the greater part of that particular food. These should be high-quality ingredients like meat (not meat by-products, a euphemism for minimally or non-nutritive parts of the food animal typically discarded by slaughterhouses, such as feet, horns, ground beaks, organ linings, etc.) or whole grains (not grain chaff or processed grains that have been stripped of certain components, like bran).

The label should also contain a guaranteed analysis chart. This breaks down the levels of protein, fat, fiber, and moisture in the food. While this information is interesting, it doesn't indicate much about the food's quality. What's important is the nutritional value of the ingredients, not the moisture content.

Life was much easier when we just grabbed the least expensive can of wet dog food off the supermarket shelf and doled it out to our dogs. So was grabbing the cheapest brand of

---

Want to Know More?

For more information on nutrition basics, see Chapter 7: Boxer Nutritional Needs.

The Do's and Don'ts of Feeding Your Boxer Puppy

The food that's best for your dog is not always the cheapest, handiest, or most convenient. But you are committed to giving your Boxer puppy the best care possible, so you will make the effort to find the right formula for his balanced diet.

Let's start with the basics:

- DO see that your puppy's food is tasty, or he won't eat it!
- DO read nutrition labels of commercial dog foods and choose a good-quality, nutrient-balanced food. Avoid foods with chemical preservatives like BHT and ethoxyquin, which are suspected carcinogens. Look for natural preservatives like vitamin E or food without preservatives at all. Consult labels of preservative-free foods for proper storage.
- DO be consistent with the kind of food you choose, as long as it's satisfactory. A sudden change in diet can upset a dog's digestive system.
- DO ensure that fresh, clean, cool water is available at all times.
- DON'T overfeed. Your breeder and/or veterinarian can advise you on the proper amounts and frequency of meals. While some Boxers may stop eating when they're full, don't count on yours to do so.
- DON'T feed table scraps. Dogs' bodies are not constructed like ours and therefore do not have the same nutritional needs nor process food in the same way as humans do. Some ubiquitous people foods, such as chocolate and onions, are toxic to dogs. Meat bones, other than cooked beef knuckle bones, can splinter and cause serious injury to your dog's digestive tract.
- DON'T jump from brand to brand.
- DON'T overdo doggy treats. They should supplement your puppy's diet, not replace it.

peanut butter, loaded with added sugar and trans fats, and doling it out to our kids. We've come a long way in nutritional know-how, and our pets deserve to benefit from it as much as we do. Responsible dog ownership means taking all possible steps to ensure his physical and emotional health. When you're doing everything correctly, you'll know it. The proof is in the puppy.

What Type of Food Should I Use for My Puppy?

The most important consideration in feeding a puppy is that the food is nutritionally balanced and complete. It doesn't matter whether you feed a home-cooked diet or puppy kibble, as long as the food provides the puppy with the right nutrients he needs to grow and thrive.

Commercial puppy food presents many choices: kibble, wet food, and all meat. Regardless of type, commercial dog food labels should specify the life stages for which it is appropriate. Labels that say "nutritionally balanced for puppies" or "for all life stages" indicate food that is formulated with a puppy's nutritional needs in mind.

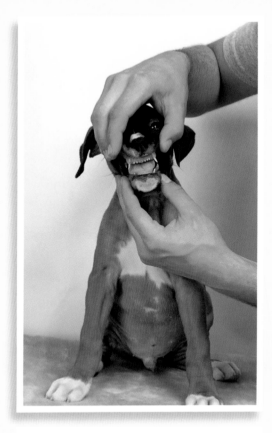

Grooming your puppy is an excellent opportunity to perform a health check.

The majority of puppyhood is high maintenance, so enjoy this respite from the intense grooming required of other breeds. Indulge your senses in the sweet smell and downy fur reserved for puppies. It will be a pleasant memory to recall when you're bathing your adult, who has just acted on his instinct to roll in rodent feces.

Grooming as Bonding Time

Not only does grooming accustom your puppy to being handled all over, it builds trust between you, furthering the bonding process. Your Boxer will rely on you for everything he needs; let him know early on that you are a capable and loving pack leader.

Grooming as a Health Check

Regular grooming is an excellent opportunity to perform a health check. Your puppy's coat may not need brushing, but running your hands down his body and limbs will alert you to any unusual bumps, growths, or external parasites on his skin. Look at his skin for any lesions or lacerations. Examine his eyes for any unusual discharge or inflammation. Normal mucus secreted from the eyes should be clear; if you notice a yellow, green, bloody, or even unusually abundant colorless discharge from the eyes, consult your veterinarian immediately.

Check the outside of your puppy's ears, a favorite site for ticks to homestead. Gently lift the ear flaps and look inside—there should be no discharge or unpleasant odor emanating from the ear. If your puppy scratches, paws, or rubs his ears on the carpet or upholstery, an infection may be causing his discomfort. Consult your vet right away.

If you opt for a raw or home-cooked diet for your puppy, you will need to become an expert on dog nutrition to ensure that you're providing everything a puppy needs. Ask your vet or breeder for information and resources.

GROOMING YOUR PUPPY

The Boxer is a low-maintenance breed, and young puppies don't venture far enough into the world to get very dirty. Puppy grooming mandates are limited to nail trimming, but it's wise to begin a general grooming regimen with your baby.

How to Get Your Puppy Used to Grooming

Fortunately for Boxers, grooming usually translates into glorified petting. Fortunately for owners, Boxers love physical interaction with their humans. Handling a puppy's paws, fingering his toes, and lifting and gently stroking his ears can all be pleasant touches he lovingly receives while in your lap. From there, transition to actual grooming is easy.

Grooming Supplies

You won't need many grooming supplies for your young puppy. A soft-bristle brush, a mild dog shampoo formulated for puppies, and a pair of toenail clippers or grinding tool are all you need on hand. Dog nail clippers come in two varieties: a guillotine-type action and ordinary shear-cut action. Both perform well; it's a matter of personal preference. Some people like the guillotine-type clippers for puppies' soft nails because it conforms more to the nail's curve. As the dog ages, his nails will become too thick for this type of clippers, and the shear-type clippers, appropriately sized for a Boxer, are more practical.

Finding a vet is the first step to taking care of your puppy's health.

You may also wish to dedicate a pair of eyebrow tweezers to the task of tick removal. Regular tick checks during grooming will reveal any uninvited guests, and tweezers are a handy tool for removal (when used properly to avoid squeezing open a blood-engorged tick).

PUPPY HEALTH

Your puppy's health is crucial to his development into a healthy adult dog. You should regard it with the same care you take of your own health.

Finding a Vet

The first step in taking care of your puppy's health is finding a veterinarian. You'll want to complete this important task before bringing your puppy home.

If you've never owned a dog, you may not know how to go about finding the right vet, because the vet in closest geographical proximity may not be the best one for your dog. If you've obtained your Boxer from a local breeder, ask which vet she uses. Chances are that if the breeder trusts a particular vet with her dogs, you can too. There's no rule stating that you must continue to use the same vet as the breeder does, but there are advantages to doing so. The pup's medical records are already established, and the vet is already familiar with your puppy. The ideal vet has hands-on experience with Boxers.

Other local Boxer owners you may know who value their dogs' well-being are good resources of information. If you're new to an area, ask the American Animal Hospital

A puppy's skin is his largest organ and reveals much about his health.

Trimming Your Puppy's Nails

Regular, gentle handling of your puppy's paws will serve you well during a lifetime of nail trimming. Dogs generally do not like their paws handled, which can make toenail trimming challenging and traumatic. From the very first, gently finger your pup's paws whenever you cuddle him. The more accustomed he becomes to having them handled, the more cooperative he will be during trimming. This is especially true if you plan to use an automatic grinding tool, like a Dremel, that painlessly files down the nail tip. The tool makes noise to which the puppy must also become accustomed, so early introduction is wise. After your puppy seems comfortable with having his paws handled, show him the grinding tool while it's turned off. Let him sniff and investigate it. Show him where you will be applying the tool for trimming.

Once he's familiar with the tool itself, try turning it on a few feet (m) away from the pup. Accustom him to the noise from a distance. If he approaches you to investigate the source of the sound, turn off the tool while he sniffs it. When safe to do so, turn it back on while he's still present. Show him that the harmless noise that comes from this harmless object will be part of his regular grooming regimen.

When he appears at ease with the tool and its noise, gently apply the tool to one toenail for a second or two, talking soothingly. As he becomes comfortable with the situation, increase the length of sanding time and the number of nails trimmed in one session. Soon he will trust you enough to allow you to perform this important grooming task without protest.

Association (AAHA) for a list of affiliated animal hospitals in your area. You might also contact the American Boxer Club (ABC), which can refer you to local Boxer clubs that will be happy to steer you in the direction of a reputable veterinarian.

Once you've obtained a few referrals, visit the offices. Arrange a consultation appointment—without your dog—with the veterinarian to whom you've been referred. When you arrive at the facility, look around the waiting and reception areas. Are they clean, organized, and up to date? Do the people and pets waiting there appear comfortable in their surroundings? Is the staff friendly, calm, and professional?

When you meet with your veterinarian, have a list of questions ready that include:

- How many vets belong to the practice?
- When was the practice first established?
- Are there any practitioners particularly knowledgeable about Boxers?
- Is the facility attended 24 hours a day by a trained staff member?
- Does the practice maintain relationships with veterinary specialists in the area?
- What are the hours of operation, and where is the closest veterinary emergency clinic?
- Are the support staff trained, compassionate veterinary technicians?
- How are patients evaluated before anesthesia and surgery?
- What is their pain management protocol? Most veterinarians will appreciate the

interest and be glad to show you their facilities and answer all questions. If you sense otherwise, move on to another office.

The First Checkup

Regular physical examinations play an important role in your Boxer's long-term health care plan. It is usually during these exams that a vet picks up early warning signs of a serious issue that may affect the dog in the future. Early detection is your Boxer's best chance for correcting an acute problem or at least slowing its progress. That first all-important puppy checkup will be comprehensive, so it helps to know what to expect.

Abdomen

The vet will palpate (gently press and feel) the dog's abdomen for lumps, abnormal distention, or possible infections. She will also pay attention to any signs of pain from the dog, which indicate further problems.

Back and Tail

The vet will visually inspect, then run her hand down the dog's spine and tail to check for any spinal problems, like intervertebral disk disease (IDD), which is sometimes seen in Boxers.

Ears

The vet will use an *otoscope*, a handheld instrument, to look inside these infamous bacteria harbors. She will also look for ear mites, a highly transmittable parasite that can make your dog miserable. Discharge, foul smell, or inflammation can indicate infection.

Eyes

Dull, lifeless eyes are the first sign that something is wrong. The condition of the

Multi-Dog Tip

In a multi-dog household, grooming sessions can be special one-on-one time with each dog. Take him to a private area, like a laundry room or back porch so that the other dog(s) won't interfere, or crate the other(s) while you groom him.

eyes can indicate stress, internal parasites, or a more serious illness. The vet will check for any debris or discharge, as contagious eye infections often start with discharge from the eye corners.

Heart

A dog's normal heartbeat ranges from 100 to 130 beats per minute. Any abnormality is cause for concern. As with most diseases, early detection of heart disease is a dog's best chance for a longer, more comfortable life.

Lungs

The vet will listen for any congestion or abnormal breathing patterns with a stethoscope. Chest congestion can indicate diseases like bordetella (kennel cough), distemper, or even heartworm.

Mouth

The mouth will be checked for lumps, cuts, or scrapes, and the condition of the teeth will be inspected as well. Healthy teeth should look clean and white; the gums should be a deep pink. Lumps may indicate an abscessed tooth, oral tumors, or an allergic reaction from an insect bite.

Nose

A cold, wet nose is not the legendary indicator of canine good health. Healthy Boxers' noses are often dry because their tongues don't always reach that high on the muzzle. Abnormal nasal discharge, however, could indicate distemper, a respiratory infection, or any number of diseases.

Paws

The paws will be examined for any cuts or swelling.

Skin and Coat

The skin is the largest organ of the body and reveals much about a dog's health. The vet will check the coat and skin for fleas, ticks, and other external parasites, as well as any swelling, abrasions, scaly patches, lumps, and general coat condition. A healthy dog has a shiny, even coat.

Vaccinations

Long considered a crucial part of preventive veterinary medicine, vaccination against disease is sometimes required by law, as with rabies. The topic of elective vaccinations has been controversial for quite a few years and is something that should be discussed with your vet. Some dog owners believe that undergoing elective vaccinations does more harm than good. Other owners believe that if their dog spends minimal time outdoors, he doesn't have enough contact with the outside world to be at risk for disease. Assuming that responsible owners realize that Boxers shouldn't be exclusively "inside dogs," it's fair to say that Boxers benefit from vaccination. Multiple-disease vaccines, such as the DHLPP combination that protects against distemper, hepatitis, leptospirosis, parvovirus, and parainfluenza (kennel

cough), are a practical and convenient way to armor your Boxer against these serious illnesses. Even though relatively few preventable diseases are fatal, they can make your dog very uncomfortable or even permanently diminish his quality of life.

Vaccinations against the following are the best way to keep your beautiful Boxer feeling as well as he looks.

Canine Bordetellosis

Also known as bordetella or kennel cough, this disease is caused by a bacterial infection of the respiratory tract. Symptoms resemble a bad cold and include a runny nose and hacking cough. Treatment includes isolating the dog to prevent spread of infection and resting in a humid environment. Run a vaporizer or humidifier in your dog's sleeping area and encourage him to nap there. The illness should run its course in about two weeks.

Spaying or neutering your Boxer will help reduce the dog overpopulation problem.

diarrhea, cough, anorexia, fever, nasal discharge, inflamed eyes, and lethargy. Treatment at the first sign of distemper greatly improves the dog's chances for recovery. Dogs with full-blown cases sometimes survive but often with permanent brain or nervous system damage.

Leptospirosis
Leptospirosis is caused by a microorganism often carried by rats. Symptoms include bloody stool or urine, fever, depression, red eyes and mouth, painful mouth sores, vomiting, thirst, anorexia, and pain. Quick treatment with antibiotics is necessary. Acute cases may need hospitalization.

Lyme Disease
Lyme disease is a bacterium spread to dogs and humans through infected tick bites. Symptoms include joint pain, fatigue, fever, skin rash. Symptoms appear about two months after infection, and treatment typically includes antibiotics and pain relievers. Recovery time depends on the severity of the case and how early it was detected.

Parainfluenza
Parainfluenza is caused by several different viruses and a bacterium. It is not overtly dangerous, but it is highly contagious among dogs. Symptoms include a hacking cough.

Coronavirus
Coronavirus is an infection of the intestinal lining that is transmitted through feces. Symptoms include lethargy, decreased appetite, and sudden diarrhea that is orange tinted, malodorous, and possibly bloody. Treatment may include IV fluids to combat dehydration and antibiotics to prevent secondary bacterial infections.

Distemper
Distemper is the number-one killer of unvaccinated dogs. Symptoms include

Treatment is antibiotics to prevent complications and medicine to ease coughing.

Parvovirus

Parvovirus was only discovered in dogs in 1977. It is believed to be a mutated strain of feline distemper. Symptoms include depression and anorexia, followed by vomiting, diarrhea, and fever. Treatment varies with the symptoms and severity of the disease, as well as the dog's age. Hospitalization is usually necessary. Your dog will probably receive medication to control vomiting and diarrhea, antibiotics to control secondary infections, and fluids to counteract dehydration.

Rabies

Rabies is transmitted by warm-blooded animals and is highly contagious to humans and animals through infected saliva. Symptoms include change in disposition, pupil dilation leading to light intolerance, coordination difficulty, facial tics, random biting, loss of facial muscle control, and coma. There is no effective treatment for this fatal disease, underscoring the importance of prevention.

Puppy-Specific Illnesses

Once a puppy is taken to a new environment, he is exposed to a host of possible ailments, many of them stress related. These common problems can occur no matter where you obtained your puppy, so they are not necessarily a negative reflection on the seller.

Kennel Cough/Upper Respiratory Infection/ Pneumonia

The same symptoms we experience during our own upper respiratory infections (URIs) can also indicate a respiratory infection in puppies. Despite vaccination, there's a 50 percent chance that a puppy will contract kennel cough. Treatment with the proper antibiotics at the first sign of illness is the best course to follow.

Diarrhea

Diarrhea can occur from stress, changes in food and water, or any environmental change. Given that puppies usually experience these stressors upon going to their new home, it's not unusual for a pup to have a bout of diarrhea. The vet will most likely request a stool sample to rule out giardia or other intestinal parasites. If tests are negative and the diarrhea continues, the vet may suggest a small amount of an over-the-counter digestive medicine like Pepto-Bismol. Be sure to consult your vet before giving your puppy any home remedy.

Hypoglycemia/Juvenile Hypoglycemia

Hypoglycemia (low blood sugar) and juvenile hypoglycemia (low blood sugar in puppies younger than three months) are the most common metabolic disorders seen in young puppies. They are at greater risk for it than adult dogs because they have a smaller

Training Tidbit

Clicker training, a popular method of positive reinforcement that uses a clicking sound to mark desired behavior when it's performed, is effective because it involves association with a sound that the dog doesn't hear in his daily routine .

Spaying or neutering your Boxer will help reduce the dog overpopulation problem.

liver, less muscle, and a larger brain in proportion to body size. They cannot store very much sugar in their muscles and liver for later use, and may exhibit signs of deficiency like weakness, dizziness, confusion, fainting, and even convulsions. These symptoms most often appear first thing in the morning, after the puppy has fasted all night, or after periods of intense play or stress. Your vet will probably advise feeding several high-calorie, high-fat, and high-protein puppy-food meals per day.

Blood/Mucus in the Stool

Blood or mucus in the stool can be a sign of intestinal parasites. Blood in the stool can also indicate viral infection or intestinal blockage. If you see any blood or gelatinous mucus in your puppy's stool, consult a veterinarian right away.

Spaying/Neutering

One of the many reasons you need to closely examine your expectations of Boxer ownership is the dog's reproductive life. Unless you plan to become seriously involved in conformation and breeding, you will need to consider spaying or neutering your Boxer before reaching adolescence and before it goes through its first estrus period.

There are many good reasons to spay or neuter your Boxer:

• dog overpopulation
• prevention of disease of reproductive organs
• avoiding the heightened behaviors of heat and rut cycles

Altering your Boxer is a decision that should give you peace of mind, knowing that your dog will not be contributing to pet overpopulation or be subjected to certain diseases. Veterinarians perform these surgeries so often that you need not feel any reservations about deciding to have your dog spayed or neutered. If cost is an issue, many animal shelters sponsor spay/neuter clinics where veterinary professionals perform the surgeries for a lower price than private veterinary practices.

Neutering

Adolescent male dogs experience raging hormones as they approach maturity. The mating instinct drives them to follow, at all costs, the scent of a female in heat. Rutting male Boxers have been known to jump over 6-foot (2-m) fences and break through screened enclosures in pursuit of a local female in estrus. Intact males also present the challenge of natural selection: competition with other males for the prize. "Survival of the fittest" dictates that the strongest, most dominant male will succeed in mating with the female(s) in season. Male aggression with other males is much more likely in an intact male than in a neutered one.

Neutering a male dog involves removing the testes, a less complex surgery than female hysterectomy, and neutering can be performed on dogs as young as six months. An overnight stay at the animal hospital is usually unnecessary. The dog is in no way compromised by the surgery, other than in his ability to breed. Considering the number of unwanted, homeless dogs in the world, this is a good thing.

If you've purchased a pet-quality male Boxer puppy from a reputable breeder, she may ask you to sign a contract stipulating that you will not breed the dog and will have him duly neutered. The breeder is not behaving pretentiously; she is a professional who understands that only those Boxers who most closely conform to the breed standard should produce offspring to perpetuate good health and temperament. A pet-quality Boxer may have a muzzle slightly longer than it should be or have more than the one-third white coloration (flash) permitted by the breed standard. If he comes from a responsible breeder, though, he is no more likely to develop any medical problems than his show-quality littermates. In the interest of breed improvement, a breeder does not want to perpetuate a bloodline with substandard physical or temperamental features.

Spaying

A female Boxer (called a *bitch*) who will not be bred typically undergoes a complete hysterectomy at around one year of age. Popular belief has held that a female spayed before her first estrus is at a lower risk for breast cancer. Spaying should not take place at too young an age lest the puppy be deprived of hormones needed for proper growth. The advantage of spaying? No seasonal muss, no fuss, and no rutting males at your door.

Surgical spaying of a female is a more involved procedure than neutering a male. An overnight hospital stay is sometimes required, but most spayed females go home the same day and experience no complications. Healthy bitches recover quickly and can live the rest of their lives free from the risk of cancer in their reproductive organs.

CHAPTER 4

TRAINING YOUR BOXER PUPPY

Training a dog is really no different from teaching manners to your child. A youngster doesn't know what behavior is socially acceptable; neither does a puppy. He must be properly socialized, acknowledge his humans as authority figures, and learn to be interesting and enjoyable company. A properly trained Boxer is self-confident, his owner is proud, and both have forged a lifelong bond to each other.

While the ABC may not endorse specific practitioners, they can provide you with names and addresses in your area. Another helpful resource is the American Animal Hospital Association (AAHA), which can provide a list of affiliated veterinarians in your area. Realtors are also good sources for vet referrals; it's their job to know the community and its services. Once you have some names, you can visit the practices and evaluate their suitability yourself.

INTRODUCTION TO TRAINING

It's been said that owning an untrained dog is like owning a piano without ever having learned how to play it. Training is especially important to a breed like the Boxer.

Why Is Training Important?

When humankind decided to integrate dogs into their world, they undertook the obligation to teach them how to function successfully in that world. Combine a strong, muscular dog with intelligence and curiosity and you get a dog who needs training, even more so than other breeds. Without it, the Boxer's brute strength and rough play could get him into all sorts of trouble. All dogs need training and socialization to help them learn about and cope with the world around them. This becomes even more important for a breed genetically—albeit primordially—linked with dogs traditionally portrayed as vicious and used for fighting.

Resolve to give your Boxer puppy the best training available. If you adopt an older puppy, find out if he's received training while in his former home. If not, it may take a little more patience and persistence to unlearn bad habits, but it's imperative that the dog learn acceptable behavior. Owning an untrained Boxer means, at best, owning a dog who will never reach his potential as a companion. At worst, it spells disaster. Imagine a strong, uncontrollable dog in a social environment. The picture isn't pretty.

The Importance of Positive Training

Positive training simply means rewarding desired behavior, not punishing bad behavior. In fact, the word "punish" should not be in a dog owner's vocabulary because it is never appropriate to hit, yell at, isolate, or withhold food and water from a dog. Discipline, on the other hand, is a means of obtaining desired behavior and discouraging unwanted behavior. That's where positive training comes in.

It's fair to say that most dogs are highly food motivated, so treat rewards for desired behavior achieve the quickest results. Keep the treat small. The time taken to divide a large treat into small bits or chew and swallow a crunchy bone negates training efficacy. The treat should be immediately offered when the dog performs the desired behavior so that he associates the action with the reward. Moreover, smaller treats mean fewer calories. Positive training is not an excuse to overindulge your Boxer.

Edible treats are not the only rewards suitable for positive training. A dog who performs a desired action can have a few minutes with a favorite toy, or a romp with you. Your affection and pleasure are the best rewards a Boxer can enjoy.

How to Find a Trainer

Ask the breeder from whom you obtained your Boxer if she knows any trainers, or which trainer she uses. If you know of other Boxer owners, ask them as well. The ideal trainer, like an ideal vet, will have hands-on experience with the breed. Try to find a trainer who suits not only your personality, but your philosophy as well.

Before you sign on with any trainer, ask if you may observe her conducting a class, preferably a puppy class. Watch how she interacts with the puppies and their humans. Is she patient? Does she provide clear instructions? Does she advocate and practice compassionate discipline?

If a trainer refuses to let you observe her at work, she has something to hide. Continue your search for the right trainer.

SOCIALIZATION

Not unlike humans, dogs are social animals who, in the wild, live and thrive in groups with distinct social hierarchies of their own. Socialization for us, however, means something different than it does for domesticated dogs.

What Is Socialization?

Where we might socialize by interacting with one another in a recreational setting, socializing a puppy involves exposing him to all of the sights and sound he is likely to encounter, inside and outside, during his life with you. These include people of different genders, races, sizes, ages, and

By the Numbers

A puppy is ready for training as soon as you take him home (no earlier than eight weeks of age), and his first lesson will no doubt be housetraining. Give him about a week to adjust to his new home, then enroll him in "puppy kindergarten," a group training class where he will learn basic obedience and important socialization skills.

physical abilities, and the sights and sounds of everyday life like cars, trucks, buses, lawn mowers, and bicycles. Keep in mind that the world can be awfully intimidating to a young puppy accustomed to the familiar, cozy cloister of his mother and littermates. Sensible socialization starts small and works up to large, loud things and people. There are limits though: Thunderstorms and fireworks can be frightening to even the most thoroughly socialized dog.

HOW TO SOCIALIZE

Socializing must be performed early in a puppy's life to be effective. Once he has had all of the necessary shots and won't be exposed to anything potentially harmful, you can begin the enjoyable task of socializing.

You can combine socializing with leash-walking practice and other commands your puppy will have learned later in this chapter, although it's best not to combine socialization with training basic obedience commands. But practice makes perfect, so leash walking in your neighborhood is a good way to introduce your baby Boxer to all kinds of people in your community.

If you're at a loss for socializing ideas, here are a few to get you started:

- Visit the kennel where the puppy was whelped.

- Take him with you in public to meet people who will stop to admire and coo over your pup.

- Allow children of different age groups to play with him, under careful adult supervision.

- Take your puppy to parks and shops that welcome dogs.

- Introduce him to people you may know who use canes, walkers, and wheelchairs.

- Expose him to bicycle and motorcycle riders, inline skaters, and skateboarders.

- Introduce him to the neighbors, who are good resources for help in this step.

- Take him to a facility where people ride horses.

CRATE TRAINING

The very words "crate training" have the unsavory connotation of imprisonment, but in fact, a dog's crate is his castle. Dogs are denning animals by nature, and they prefer to curl up in small areas that give them a sense of protection. When used appropriately and with proper training, the crate will provide security and comfort for your puppy and peace of mind for you.

What Is Crate Training?

Crate training means gradually adapting your Boxer to temporary confinement without anxiety in his crate. To confine a dog in a crate without proper training is unfeeling and inefficient. All a puppy knows is that he's been removed from the security and familiarity of his mother and littermates; he won't understand why you've further isolated him by shutting him away in a strange "den." You must convince your puppy that the crate is not a prison but a pleasant, cozy den where he is safe and content.

Benefits of Crate Training

When a puppy is about five weeks old, he will start toddling away from his mother and littermates to relieve himself, acting on an instinct not to soil his living area. This instinct will be useful in the housetraining of your puppy, and a crate will make the process that much easier.

Socialization includes introducing your dog to other dogs.

At the tender age of eight to ten weeks—when most puppies leave their litters for new homes—his developing bladder and bowel control will not allow him to go more than an hour or so without relieving himself. It's up to you to make sure that he isn't left inside his crate for too long.

There will be times when you are unable to supervise your puppy, even while at home. At these times, the crate will prevent him from soiling all over the house. It will also keep him out of mischief; you want him safe from potential hazards while you're unable to watch him.

Dogs instinctively refrain from soiling their sleeping areas, which is why the crate is such an important tool in housetraining. But a puppy has limited control over his immature bowels and bladder. It's unrealistic to crate him for more than an hour without the likelihood of soiling, even if he has already learned to enjoy being in his crate.

Remember that crating your puppy while at home and crating him before you leave home are very different scenarios. He may need remedial training to understand that you are not leaving forever—that you will return and take him out of his crate. Start with walks around the block, gradually building up the time you stay out of the house. Keep departures and arrivals free of drama. Leaving a radio or television on during your absences can be soothing.

HOW TO CRATE TRAIN
It may take a little while for your puppy to recognize the crate as his own special refuge, so it's a good idea to introduce the crate to him before you actually need to confine him

in it. Prepare the crate by lining the bottom with thick layers of newspaper to act as a cushion and absorb accidents. Prop open the crate door and toss a treat inside, saying "Crate" or "Bed" as you do this. Allow him to go inside for the treat, sniff around a bit, and exit the crate when he's ready. Leave the door open to allow him to come and go at will.

When he seems comfortable with it, serve his next meal inside the crate. Keep the door open as he eats, then progress to closing the door once he's gone inside to eat. When he's finished, let him out of the crate and immediately take him outside to relieve himself. Pretty soon, he will learn that the crate isn't a prison but a cozy nook where good things are to be had.

The hard part comes at bedtime. Your new Boxer will no doubt cry the first night or two that he goes to bed alone in his crate, but this is normal. After all, until now he's spent his sleeping hours surrounded by the comfort of his littermates. Resist the temptation to let him out of the crate when he cries. Say "Quiet!" in a firm voice or simply close the door to the room and leave. If you give in to his crying and let him out, he'll learn that tantrums yield positive results. You want him to learn that he may come out of the crate only when he's quiet and you are ready.

Crate Location
The location of the crate goes a long way toward a decent night's sleep for both you and your new puppy. Try placing the crate in your bedroom near the bed. With you nearby, your puppy will have a sense of security. If you hear him whine or scratch at the crate door in the middle of the night, he most likely needs to relieve himself. Taking him outside at these times will speed up the housetraining process and bring you closer to that first night of

undisturbed sleep. Praise him when he does his business, then put him back into the crate. If he still whines or acts up, rap on top of the crate with the reprimand "Quiet!"

During the day when your puppy looks tired, put him in the crate for a nap with the door shut. This will help him learn that his crate is his place to sleep.

Crate Size
Although your puppy will eventually grow into a large dog, and you will need a size-appropriate crate, you don't want to start off with a big one while your Boxer is still very young. If the crate is too large, he will quickly discover that he can eliminate at one end of the crate without soiling a good portion of bedding space. It makes more sense to start with a smaller crate and upsize as he grows. A good rule of thumb when crate shopping is that it should be large enough for the dog to stand up and turn around comfortably. If you must start off with a larger size crate, partition off half of it to reduce the available space.

HOUSETRAINING
The first thing to understand about teaching your Boxer where to appropriately

Multi-Dog Tip

Training individual dogs in a multi-dog home enables you to focus the training session on one dog while providing quality "alone" time with him. Once all of the dogs in your pack are trained for the routines of your household, start working with them as a group.

relieve himself is the reason it's not called "housebreaking." You will not be "breaking" your puppy's will or bad habit, neither of which relate to elimination practices.

What Is Housetraining?

"Housetraining" means teaching your puppy in a positive way the location in which you wish him to eliminate. This training begins as soon as you bring him home, but don't expect too much; his bladder and bowel control is still immature. He will quickly learn where you want him to go, but his body will take some time to catch up. Puppies also mature at varying rates; some require more time than others to learn. Practice patience.

How to Housetrain

Some people prefer to start housetraining their Boxer with paper training. This makes sense for city or apartment dwellers who don't have ready access to an outside elimination spot. When possible, however, it's preferable to directly proceed with outdoor potty training.

Before you bring your puppy home for the first time, ask his breeder if you may collect some urine-soaked litter from his living area in a sealable plastic bag. Scatter this used litter around the outdoor site where your pup will relieve himself at your home. The scent will identify the site to him as the proper place to go.

Upon arriving home with your new pup, go immediately to the outdoor elimination site. Put him down where you've spread the litter and wait patiently until he urinates and/or defecates. (This may take some time.) Lavish praise on him when he succeeds, convincing him that you couldn't be more pleased.

Over the next weeks, keep an eye out for telltale signals that your puppy needs to eliminate. If he walks around sniffing the floor, he's searching for the scent that tells him he's found the right place. Take him outside right away, and praise him when he does his business. If you don't catch him in time, and he's already begun to eliminate, immediately remove him outside *without* an emotional reaction. The interruption may require a few extra minutes before he resumes eliminating, but wait patiently and show him your approval when he finishes. Always take him out after eating, drinking, or sleeping, cheering him on when he relieves himself in the correct spot.

It's a fact of life: Accidents will happen. When they do, never punish your Boxer by striking him or rubbing his nose in his mistake. This only conveys your displeasure that he eliminated, not because he did so in the wrong place. Chastising after the fact will only confuse your puppy. He will learn to mistrust you, thereby sabotaging any training efforts you make thereafter.

BASIC OBEDIENCE

Basic obedience is important for all dogs but especially so for Boxers. A breed of his size and strength needs to be in your control at all times, for his own safety as well as for the safety of those around him. It's worth repeating that positive reinforcement for desired behavior—not punishment for mistakes—is the key to successful training.

Before you embark on a training program, think about what your goals are for your Boxer. Do you want a well-mannered, calm home-body? Do you want him to be well behaved beyond immediate family and home turf? Do you aspire to dog sports and competitions? Regardless of future goals, basic obedience is the foundation of every well-adjusted companion dog.

The first commands you and your Boxer will master are *sit*, *come*, and *down*. He must

To make your puppy feel more secure, try placing the crate in your bedroom near the bed.

The Golden Rule of Crates

Never use the crate as a place of punishment. You want your puppy to like his crate and consider it his home within a home. If your puppy has an accident or gets into mischief and you need to remove him to a safe place while you attend to other things, make sure you distinguish the crate from your displeasure before placing him in it. Take him outside for a bathroom break; your return inside will be a fresh start.

also learn to walk on a leash. Because your priority is total control of you Boxer at all times, these commands work well to that end. And of course, a well-mannered dog is always preferable to an undisciplined, hyperactive pet.

Sit

The simple *sit* is a good jumping-off place for every subsequent command you will give your dog. It's also a good command to teach first because a puppy already knows how to sit. The trick is to get him to do it when *you* want him to do it. Entice him with a treat held just above and in front of his face; his eyes and head will automatically raise to follow it and his rear should naturally assume a *sit*. Be sure that the verbal command is given at precisely the same moment as his head goes up and his rear

goes down. He will quickly learn what you want and when you want him to do it. End every training session on a positive note with a nicely executed *sit*, rewarded by a treat, and his self-confidence will blossom.

Come

This command can save the life of a dog who may have eluded supervision or containment and is heading toward an open road or a wild animal. Believe it or not, the *come* command is more challenging than you'd think. It takes little time to get your Boxer to come to you when called, but it is a command that can be easily untaught via misuse.

There are two simple ways to teach your puppy to come. The first is with a long lead that you gradually gather in your hands to bring him toward you while saying "Come!" A more realistic method is to kneel down, hold your arms wide open, and enthusiastically

Never punish your Boxer if he has an accident in the house.

say "Come!" Praise him to the skies when he does. That's all there is to it. But there are a few important points to remember about this command:

- NEVER call your Boxer to come to you and punish him. Association of the command with anything negative unravels all training purposes in one fell swoop.

- Don't overwork the command by calling him to you too frequently.

- Spring an unexpected "Come!" on him when he is distracted by another activity, such as playing. You want him to learn to heed your call no matter what else he might be doing.

- Remember to always reward him for coming to you, whether it's with a treat or very enthusiastic praise.

Down

This command requires the pup to lie down on his belly and stay there, an important submissive position used when you want to emphasize to him that you are in charge. Because Boxers can sometimes be dog-aggressive, training them to assume and maintain a *down-stay* position while another dog passes by is useful in preventing skirmishes with other dogs. With collar and lead attached, put your dog in a *sit* position. Gently pull the leash downward with your right hand. At the same time, move your left hand in front of his face in a downward movement, like you're bouncing a ball. Say "Down" during the action. If you prefer, tuck a small treat under the thumb of your left hand as you make the downward movement. Your dog should follow the scent in your hand. If he doesn't lie down right away, slide the treat slowly on the floor away from his nose. This will encourage him to lie down

The *sit* is an easy command for a puppy to learn.

to track the treat. Eventually, he will know that the strong, downward hand movement, coupled by the verbal command, means "hit the deck." Later on, you can practice the *down-stay*, where he remains in the *down* position until released by a verbal command from you.

Leash Training

Leash training is one of the first things you both should learn, especially if you plan to participate with your Boxer in conformation. Walking nicely on a leash, without pulling, will be a part of everyday life with your Boxer, something to be enjoyed, not endured. A good time to begin leash training your puppy is when he has enough stamina for short walks, at around eight weeks. By that age, his attention span will have also increased to the point where he will benefit from the mental stimulation of training.

Any kind of collar will feel strange to your puppy at first. He will paw and scratch at it, but before long he will get used to it. Opinions differ on which type of collar is best to start off your pup's leash training with, but one of the most popular choices is the nylon show collar. This type should be used only for leash training and walking; you can go fancy or colorful with his everyday collar. You will also want to buy a leather, nylon, or cotton-webbing training lead that is about 6 feet (2 m) long. Save the chain lead or retractable leashes for post-training use.

To teach your Boxer how to walk nicely on a lead, you must first teach him to follow you off lead. Start walking him in a calm area, allowing him to explore. Show him a treat and call him to come close to you. Praise him when he does, and reward him with the treat. Encourage him to follow you as you walk for a few minutes, then release him to explore some more on his own. The goal here is to acquaint him with walking by your side off lead so that the transition to walking on lead will be easy. After he's mastered the concept of following you, it's time to move on to walking on lead.

Begin in an area the puppy has come to know well, like your own yard. The familiar smells will help him stay focused on the training session, as new scents are just too tempting to resist! Attach the lead to his collar and begin walking. Call him to you, enticing him with a treat, and he should follow you the same way he did off lead. An alternate method is to attach the lead to the pup's collar, then back away from him

with a treat in your hand. Stoop down and offer him the treat as you tell him to come. This sends a dual message: coming to his owner when called *and* following her reap tasty rewards.

PUPPY KINDERGARTEN

Your Boxer's training should start even before you bring him home, with socialization while at his breeder's. Once he goes home with you, you take over this responsibility. This doesn't mean that you are on your own completely; it just means that your first act as a responsible Boxer owner is to find and enroll your puppy in a puppy training class, or puppy kindergarten. Although you can't expect to see results from training until your Boxer's a little more mature, you can begin teaching him where you want him to eliminate, what chewing behavior is acceptable, and a measure of temporary independence away from family.

> ### Want to Know More?
>
> To teach your Boxer the *down-stay*, see Chapter 9: Boxer Training.

Your Boxer's training should start even before you bring him home, with socialization while at his breeder's.

Finding the right kindergarten class for your Boxer puppy is an important task that should not be left to chance. While you can utilize resources like the telephone book or the local newspaper, it's preferable to consult an expert. A logical place to start is with your breeder, who might be a trainer as well. If not, she will surely know of some in your area. Your veterinarian is also a good source of information on local trainers, as are other Boxer owners. No matter where you gather referrals, it's important to talk to the trainer personally and visit the facility. Is she experienced in training Boxers, whose intelligence and tenacity can sometimes make training a challenge? Ask permission to observe a puppy kindergarten class; does the trainer treat both puppies and humans with respect and kindness? Is the training "classroom" clean and appropriately fitted? Do the puppies and their humans respond positively to the trainer? Listen to your instincts. If the smallest doubt arises about anything you see or hear, keep searching. The right kindergarten will bring out the best in your Boxer pup; the wrong one can create temperament issues where there were none. Rough treatment and harsh voices can instill fear into a once-confident puppy. Make sure that the puppy kindergarten class you choose is in keeping with your goals and sensibilities.

PART II

ADULTHOOD

CHAPTER 5

FINDING YOUR ADULT BOXER

The siren call of an adorable puppy is hard to resist, and many people find the joys of puppyhood well worth the demands of puppy care. However, the advantages of adding an adult dog to the family are often overlooked.

WHY ADOPTING AN ADULT IS A GOOD IDEA

Most Boxers are considered fully mature by the age of 18 months, although some "late bloomers" may reach adulthood at two years. As any Boxer owner can attest, though, an officially mature Boxer has plenty of puppy in his spirit, and the result is often a rambunctious adolescent who doesn't know his own size and strength.

Nevertheless, adopting an adult Boxer means escaping the work and upheaval to your household that a puppy brings. Yes, you will miss the puppy breath, cuddliness, and wonderment of learning, but you'll save yourself the months of chewing, housetraining accidents, and sleep deprivation. The adult Boxer brings his own certain challenges, of course, but most people believe that the benefits outweigh them, not the least of which is one less homeless dog in the world.

ADOPTION OPTIONS

Once upon a time, "adopted" dogs were usually strays, taken into the homes of compassionate people. As animal welfare became more mainstream, the benefits of adopting a homeless dog became clearer. Now the Information Age connects adoptive families to needy dogs far and near.

Shelters

The first place that comes to mind when adopting an adult dog is the local animal shelter. Yet a certain stigma surrounds shelter dogs: They must be problematic, or they wouldn't be in a shelter, unwanted.

Nothing could be more untrue. Dogs end up in shelters for many reasons: They were strays, their owners died or could no longer care for them, or for numerous other reasons. Of course, committed dog owners know that pets are not disposable; therefore, moving,

---

Want to Know More?

For information on obtaining a puppy, see Chapter 2: Finding and Prepping for Your Puppy.

Dogs end up in shelters for many reasons through no fault of their own—adopting a Boxer or Boxer mix from a shelter could save his life.

having a baby, or other lifestyle changes are unacceptable reasons for relinquishing your dog to a shelter, where he may ultimately be euthanized if not adopted. This is why careful forethought is necessary

Multi-Dog Tip

An adult Boxer joining a multi-dog home will learn a lot of the household routine from the others. If your other dogs exhibit role-model behavior, the new dog should follow suit.

before adding any pet to your household.

Animal shelters usually have a large complement of mixed-breed dogs, but purebreds do sometimes end up in shelters. They are often disregarded for adoption due to the misconception that there must be something wrong with them that led to their being discarded. However, the sad fact is that some pet owners would rather give away their dog instead of making the effort to accommodate their needs or arrange for the dog's custody in the event of major life changes. Giving these dogs a new home is a gift to both dog and new owner.

Mixed-breed dogs who are part Boxer are often found in shelters, waiting for a new home. Keep in mind, however, that these dogs' mysterious heritages may include an unreliable temperament. If you're flexible enough to work through any physical and/or emotional issues that may arise, adopting a Boxer or Boxer mix through a shelter is a loving choice.

Rescues

Animal welfare has never been more in the forefront, as breed rescue organizations affirm. Most dog breeds have their own rescue organizations throughout the country and offer a wonderful opportunity to adopt a dog in need. Many Boxer fanciers have rescued pets from abusive or neglectful homes, acquiring loving and loyal pets in the process. Animal shelters that are short on space and reluctant to euthanize will relinquish dogs to breed rescue organizations. Be prepared to meet ownership standards set by the rescue group, who will interview you and evaluate your financial, emotional, and physical ability to adopt a rescued Boxer who may have behavioral issues resulting from his previous situation. For those with the right resources, Boxer rescue can be a rewarding means of adopting a dog into your family.

Breeders

It may surprise you to know that Boxer breeders are often a reliable source of adult Boxers up for adoption. Professional breeders usually own several dogs at once but have their individual limits on the number. A responsible breeder doesn't keep more dogs than she can provide for, or sometimes an antagonistic relationship between dogs in residence may require permanent separation. An older Boxer who has finished conformation and is past breeding age makes a wonderful companion for a family looking to bypass the hardships

Training Tidbit

Training an adult dog can actually be easier than training a puppy. An adult has a longer attention span and is calmer than an enthusiastic puppy.

of puppyhood. Selling an adult Boxer does not imply that the dog is defective.

QUESTIONS TO ASK THE SHELTER OR RESCUE

With so many homeless dogs in the world, adopting a shelter or rescued dog is a loving way to add a pet to your family. It comes with its own set of responsibilities that are not to be undertaken lightly, however. Before you actually contact a shelter or rescue organization, you should compile a list of important questions to ask staff members about any dog you consider adopting. The answers to many of these questions will not be available, but it's wise to obtain as much detailed information as possible.

- **What is the exact or estimated age of the dog?** Veterinarians are usually able to approximate a dog's age from his teeth and physicality.

- **What breed is the dog? If he's a mixed breed, which breed(s) might be part of his heritage?** This is particularly important for Boxers and Boxer mixes because of the Boxer's bully-breed origins. They are often included in breed-specific legislation, so

Many Boxer fanciers have rescued their dogs and acquired loving, loyal pets in the process.

you will want to check with your local government first.

- **How long has the dog been with the shelter or rescue organization?** Life in a shelter, although safe, can cause stress and depression in dogs who have been there a long time. With patience and love, adoptive families can bring out the best in these dogs.

- **How many owners has the dog had in his lifetime?** If he's had several, he may require more time than usual to establish trust with his "forever family."

- **Was the dog a stray, a rescue, a disaster victim, or imported from abroad?** His circumstances will determine much of his behavior and an adopted family's expectations.

- **If the dog was relinquished by his owner, why?** Did his elderly owner die? Did he have an irresponsible owner who didn't understand that dogs aren't disposable?

- **Is the dog's medical history known?** The shelter/rescue should give you all they have on the dog.

- **Does the dog have a history of abuse or neglect?** Not only is this information important to determine suitability between dog and adoptive family, it will help you navigate the adjustment period.

- **Has the dog been treated for any medical conditions while in the care of the shelter/rescue?** This is a good time to discuss any treatments that should be continued by the dog's adoptive family.

- **Has the dog displayed any temperament issues while at the shelter/rescue?** Behavioral problems such as food or toy aggression, dog aggression, human aggression, timidity, separation anxiety, intolerance of children, or excessive barking must be evaluated and discussed prior to any adoption.

- **Has the facility tested the dog's ability to get along well with other dogs and cats?** This is important especially for adoptive families with existing pets.

- **Does the dog prefer a certain kind of human?** Some dogs respond differently to certain people: male, female, elderly, bearded, uniformed, etc. Abused dogs particularly may have continuing issues with appearances they identify with their abusers.

- **Has the dog received socialization and/or training while in the care of the shelter/ rescue?** This information is important to the dog's compatibility with your family and indicates if continued socialization/ training will be needed once he joins the family.

- **Does the shelter/rescue provide adoptive families with professional support, if needed?** Does their staff include vets and trainers who can assist you with any behavioral, veterinary, or rehabilitation issues that may develop? If not, can they refer you to qualified professionals in your area?

- **What is the dog's reproductive history, if any?** This is an important component of a dog's overall health profile. It's difficult to know if a stray dog who enters a shelter/rescue has sired any litters, but a vet can conjecture about a stray bitch.

- **What is the shelter/organization's policy on spaying/neutering adopted dogs?** Most shelters/rescues will require that every dog they release for adoption first be spayed or neutered, if he hasn't already. Not only does altering guarantee that a dog cannot further contribute to an already massive pet overpopulation, it greatly reduces the chances for diseases involving the reproductive organs. To facilitate this important responsibility for as many adoptive families as possible, shelter veterinarians typically offer the procedure at a fee much lower than private animal hospitals.

- **Will the shelter/organization reclaim the dog if his new adoptive home doesn't work out for any reason?** Ideally, adoptive families examine potential conflicts *before* making the decision to add a dog to the household. Lifestyles, work schedules, allergies, home environments, finances, alternative custody arrangements must be compatible with the needs of a pet. Adding a dog to the family should never be a "we'll see" proposition regarding permanence. If, however, unforeseen circumstances prevent you from keeping your adopted dog at any point, will the shelter/rescue take him back? Already-overcrowded shelters obviously strive to educate the public that pets are not disposable, but they certainly prefer that an unwanted dog be returned to them and not abandoned or neglected.

By the Numbers

A Boxer is considered an adult around 18 months of age.

CHAPTER 6

BOXER GROOMING NEEDS

One look at a healthy Boxer is all it takes to understand why he is such a show-stopper. The expressive, intelligent eyes, shiny coat, and chiseled physique all add up to a dog who turns heads. The best part is that you don't need a lot of time and money to keep him that way.

Regular grooming does more than beautify your Boxer. It's the perfect opportunity for you to spend quality time together. Gentle brushing or combing is really just petting with a purpose. Your Boxer doesn't care if you're grooming him or not; all he knows is that you're lavishing attention on him and it feels great. With a minimum of regular care, you can bond with your Boxer and keep him looking gorgeous.

A Boxer's coat is more than attractive; it protects his skin from the elements and helps keep him warm in cold temperatures. It's also a barometer of his general health. A Boxer in good health has a glossy, clean-smelling, velvety coat. A dull, lackluster coat, with or without dandruff, may indicate a dietary deficiency or some other medical problem. Bald patches are a sure sign of trouble, usually mange or another skin ailment.

BRUSHING

Even though matting and tangling aren't issues for a Boxer, brushing should be a part of his regular grooming regime. It stimulates circulation and distributes the natural oils that protect him against the elements.

How to Brush Your Boxer

All you need is a long-handled brush with dense, soft bristles or a grooming (currying) glove. (Some professional groomers prefer brushes with natural bristles, claiming that synthetic brushes generate too much static electricity.) Remember these sensible tips:

Start at the head and follow the direction of the fur, working back toward the tail.

- Apply enough pressure to stimulate the skin but not so much that your dog is uncomfortable.

- Be extra gentle on the sensitive belly and undersides, where hair is sparse, or where there are any ticklish spots that make his skin twitch.

During shedding (usually spring and fall), when even short-coated breeds "blow their coats" to accommodate new growth, a shedding comb comes in handy. A metal loop fitted into a handle, this type of comb has a serrated edge that catches the loose undercoat. One side has small, fine teeth while the other has larger, more widely spaced teeth. The smaller side works best on a Boxer. Considering the gobs of loose hair that cling to the comb, you may want to perform this type of grooming outside.

BATHING

A Boxer won't need much bathing during his lifetime. Unless he's had unfortunate contact with something nasty or is a therapy dog (many organizations require their therapy dogs to be bathed prior to every visit), a bath won't clean off anything that regular brushing doesn't remove. Too much bathing strips the dog's skin of natural oils and can lead to uncomfortable itching or a rash. If you feel strongly about regular dog bathing, restrict baths to once a month in summer and once every two months in winter. Use only a mild dog shampoo. Human shampoos contain too much detergent and are harsh on a dog's skin. Boxers are not natural water lovers, but they will stoically endure a bath to please you. The easier you

Unless he's excessively dirty, your Boxer won't require many baths throughout his life—although he may enjoy playing with the hose!

Multi-Dog Tip

If you have several dogs in the family, make grooming a special one-on-one time with you for each dog. In addition to eliminating the distractions of other dogs, this "quality time" will reinforce the strong bond between you and your Boxer.

make bath time, the more cooperative your Boxer will be. Even if he enjoys the water, a bath is not the same as a dip at the old swimming hole. A little organization will make the experience a non-event.

How to Bathe Your Boxer

For an indoor bath, choose a warm location, free from drafts. Outdoor baths should take place only during warm weather. When the water is at a comfortably warm temperature, fill the tub with just enough to cover your dog's feet. His footing will feel more secure in just a few inches (cm) of water, rather than in the full tub that humans prefer. You may wish to use a rubber tub mat to ensure firm footing.

- Lift him into the tub by wrapping one arm around his chest and the other around the back of his legs, just below the tail. Boxers are solid dogs, so you may want to enlist someone's help if you are unable to lift your dog comfortably by yourself. Don't allow him to jump into the slippery tub.

- Once he's in the tub, give him a minute or two to adjust before wetting him down. He won't enjoy being doused before he knows what's going on. Keep a hand on him at all times to make him feel secure and prevent him from jumping out.

- If you have a handheld shower attachment, use a soft spray to wet his body. If not, use a plastic cup or bowl to scoop up water to wet down the coat, avoiding his head.

- Pour a small amount of shampoo into your hand and gently it work into his coat, taking care not to get any into his ears, eyes, nose, or mouth. Not only will the shampoo irritate those areas, but it will make an unpleasant memory that can make future baths a struggle.

- After shampooing your Boxer's body, use a warm, wet washcloth to gently wipe his face, paying special attention to any eye secretions. If soap gets into his eyes, ease the sting with a drop or two of mineral oil in the corner of each eye.

Regardless of whether or not your Boxer's ear's are cropped, they need regular attention to stay clean and healthy.

- Wipe the inside of his ear with a cotton ball (not a swab) dipped in mineral oil. Never insert anything into the inner ear that could damage delicate tissues.

- Take time to rinse shampoo away thoroughly with the spray attachment or plastic cup. Soap residue will leave your Boxer's coat dull and promote itching. Rinsing his underside can be a challenge without a spray attachment, but make the effort to remove all traces of shampoo.

- When he's ready to be lifted out of the tub, use the same hold used to put him in. Brace yourself; the first thing your Boxer will do is shake the excess water off his body, likely showering you in the process.

- Rub him with a clean, absorbent towel and keep him out of drafts until he's completely dry.

EAR CARE

Whether or not your Boxer's ears are cropped, they will need regular attention to stay clean and healthy. Routine inspection of your dog's ears allows you to spot parasites like ticks and ear mites or any irritation and/or discharge that could be a sign of infection. For Boxers who like to run through woods and underbrush, regular ear checks for burrs, cuts, and scratches are important.

How to Clean Your Boxer's Ears

Dip a cotton ball in mineral oil. Hold the ear flap with one hand and gently wipe away any surface dirt, paying special attention to the nooks and crannies of the ear without poking down inside. Don't try to clean the inner ear with a cotton swab or anything else that might damage delicate tissues. Leave that to the vet, who has the equipment and expertise to safely examine the inner ear during routine checkups.

If you think that something is lodged in your Boxer's ear, or he has an annoying wax buildup, don't attempt to remove it yourself and risk injury. Let a veterinary professional handle it.

Diagnosing Ear Problems

How do you know if your Boxer has an ear problem? His behavior is your best guide. If he frequently shakes his head, scratches his outer ear, or rubs the side of his head on the floor or furniture, take a look inside. Any redness and/ or discharge means something is going on that requires medical attention. Yeast infections, a common side effect of antibiotic medications, produce an annoying itch and cottage-cheesy, malodorous discharge. The vet will probably prescribe medicated ear drops to ease discomfort and kill the fungus. To administer ear drops, hold the ear flap gently away from the head, and drop the recommended dosage into the ear canal. Release the flap and gently massage the outside of the entire ear to work in the drops.

EYE CARE

Routine eye care is a simple yet important part of your Boxer's health care regimen. In addition to ordinary sties, allergies, and eye infections that can affect any dog at any time, Boxers experience a high incidence of corneal ulcerations, which can be uncomfortable for the dog and can lead to vision loss. They can occur unprovoked, so any demonstrated eye irritation should be investigated. Pawing the eye and rubbing the face against carpet or furniture can also indicate an irritation.

A healthy dog will normally secrete clear mucus from his eyes that you can easily wipe away with a soft tissue or damp cloth. Commercial products to remove "tear stains" (the narrow path of mucus running down the inner corner of the eye) are available

Training Tidbit

As early in his life as possible, start getting your Boxer used to having his feet handled by touching them, holding them gently, and fingering his toes whenever possible. As he allows you to do this without pulling away, praise him and offer a treat. When he lets you do this at any time, take the next step by showing him the clippers or grinding tool. Don't try to use it on his nails yet; just open and close the trimmers, or turn on and off the grinding tool so that he becomes familiar with the sight and sound. When you're ready to progress to actual nail trimming, start with just a few nails at a time, rewarding passivity with treats and praise. Work your way up to doing an entire paw, then two, then all four. Take care not to cut the quick, or you may lose all of the ground you've gained. A dog may forgive one such transgression, but more than that and he's not likely to cooperate in the future.

Routine eye care is a simple but important part of your Boxer's health care regimen.

at pet supply stores and favored by dog show participants. If the discharge appears yellowish or bloody, consult your vet right away. Eye abnormalities should never be ignored.

How to Clean Your Boxer's Eyes

- Moisten a soft cloth with warm water or commercial eye cleanser for dogs.

- Gently wipe around your Boxer's eyes while you talk soothingly to him.

- Observe the eyes for any irritation or abnormality, such as the lower eyelid turning inward or drooping outward.

How to Protect Your Boxer's Eyes

At home, take these steps to protect your Boxer's eyes:

- Make sure that his environment has no sharp objects at eye level. Outdoor environmental threats like thorny plants and air pollution are more difficult to control. but should be considered. Walk around the yard to look for protruding twigs and branches, thorns, or sharp-leaved plants like holly. Check the fence; are there wood splinters or nails sticking out at his eye level?

- Indoors, make certain that common houseplants like cactus, aloe, and snake plants pose no threats. Keep them out of your dog's reach.

- If you live in an area where smog can be a problem, consider your Boxer's eyes, as well as your own. If the air on a given day is not healthy for you, it's not good for your Boxer either. If you are a smoker, be aware that a light breeze can waft an ash right into your Boxer's eye.

- In a moving car, don't let your dog hold his head out of the open window. It's hard to deny him this simple pleasure—all those new smells just slapping him in the face!— but do it for safety's sake. Dirt and debris can accompany those tempting smells and injure his eyes.

- Dogs are subject to many of the same eye conditions as humans, including cataracts. Regular eye exams by you and your vet will minimize any problems that may develop. You want your Boxer's expressive eyes to be clear and bright for a lifetime.

NAIL TRIMMING

Dogs in the wild never had to worry about trimming their toenails. Their daily treks in search of food kept nails worn down to a practical length. Today, we must take charge of this task for our pets, whether it's accomplished during daily long walks on a hard surface or by manual trimming. Dogs generally don't like having their feet and toes handled, which can make nail care a challenge if they weren't accustomed to it in puppyhood.

Why is nail length important? If allowed to grow too long, toenails will interfere with a dog's natural gait. He'll tend to walk on the back of his feet, which can lead to splayed toes and an unattractive step. Eventually, excessively long toenails will curl under the feet and puncture the toe pads. Even moderately long nails are at risk of snagging on a tree root or other obstacle, causing a painful toe injury.

A more germane reason to be vigilant about trimming your Boxer's toenails involves the *quick*, the nail's blood supply. If the nail is cut too far down, the quick will also be cut, causing pain and bleeding. But as the nail grows longer, so does the quick, until it becomes impossible to trim the nail to a practical length without cutting the quick as well. Keeping the nails trimmed regularly, at least once a month, will prevent this problem.

Trimming Tools
The right tools will make nail trimming easy for both of you:

Clippers or Grinding Tool
If you've been trimming your adult Boxer's nails since puppyhood, you've noticed that his nails grew thicker and harder to cut as he grew up. The clippers you used then may not be the right size or type now. If you're unsure what size to use, consult your breeder or veterinarian. If you've been using a grinding tool, sometimes called a Dremel, chances are that it came with changeable surface heads for nails at different life stages.

Flashlight
If your Boxer's feet are white, the quick is fairly easy to see through his white toenails.

Want to Know More?

For more detailed information on corneal ulcerations, see Chapter 8: Boxer Health and Wellness.

Dogs who often walk on hard surfaces may need their nails trimmed less frequently than whose who don't.

In black nails, this area is more difficult to pinpoint. If you're unsure what the quick looks like or where it is, shine a flashlight directly behind the nail. The quick will appear as a darker spot where the blood vessel begins.

First Aid and Towel

In case you accidentally cut the quick and bleeding starts, stanch it with some corn starch or styptic powder (available in drug stores) applied directly to the affected nail. A soft bar of soap will also stop bleeding when the nail is pressed gently into it.

Treats

Stash a few treats in your pocket to reward compliance and cultivate a pleasant association with nail trimming.

How to Trim Your Boxer's Nails

• Choose a quiet time when your Boxer is relaxed. It's unrealistic to expect a dog to passively submit to nail trimming when he's playing or otherwise in high-energy mode. Nor should you attempt to trim nails while he is asleep. The touch will awaken him, and a startled dog will instinctively pull away, risking injury. He may learn to mistrust you as well.

- Assemble your supplies first, before you begin the process. Before you take hold of your Boxer, it's important to have everything you'll need handy.

- Be confident. Dogs are sensitive to our emotions, taking their cues from our behavior. If you're skittish about safely performing this task, your Boxer will sense it and deduce a justification for your hesitancy. Handle him gently but assertively.

- Locate the quick visually, with the flashlight if necessary. Position the clippers outside the quick and trim quickly. If you go too short and cut the quick, your Boxer will let you know in no uncertain terms with a yelp, and bleeding may occur. Err on the side of caution. If your dog has a mixture of black and white nails, use the amount trimmed off the white nails as a guide for the dark nails. If you're using a grinding tool, quickly pass the rotating head back and forth over the nail, using light pressure and following the nail's natural curve.

- Praise and reward. Always end nail trimming on a positive note so that your Boxer will remember nail trimming as an activity that culminates in treats.

DENTAL CARE

A dog's teeth are very strong—much sturdier than humans'—with a thick layer of enamel to protect against decay. They still require attention, however, and canine dental care has become much more proactive in recent years, resulting in healthier mouths for our dogs. Dogs in the wild usually have no dental problems because chewing the bones and ligaments of their prey naturally removes plaque from tooth surfaces (one of the reasons many dog owners feed a raw diet).

Domesticated dogs must rely on their humans to compensate.

Beyond the cosmetic benefits of white teeth and fresher breath, good dental care is imperative to your Boxer's general health. Plaque, the sticky film that constantly accumulates and hardens on teeth, contains bacteria that can spread and grow below the gum line. Bacterial toxins can lead to gingivitis, or gum inflammation. Without veterinary treatment, gingivitis can lead to periodontitis, inflammation of the tissues and/or bone surrounding the affected teeth. The body's autoimmune response to chronic inflammation causes the tissue and bone supporting the teeth to break down, resulting in pockets where the gum recedes.

By the Numbers

Dogs are born with dewclaws, vestigial nails of the fifth toe on each front pastern, that section of leg below the front knee joint. Dewclaws are a prime location for snagging. Even if kept trimmed, they can catch and tear off entirely, an extremely painful injury that can turn serious if infection sets in. To preclude this problem, most breeders have puppies' dewclaws surgically removed when they are days old. Although an unpleasant-sounding prospect, the procedure has no lingering, traumatic effect on puppies, any more than circumcision has on male human infants.

These open spaces are highly susceptible to infection. Periodontal disease can become systemic, causing increased inflammation levels throughout the body, making your Boxer ill. Even worse, high inflammation levels are a known risk factor for heart disease.

An oral health regimen is best started when your Boxer is a puppy, as he must learn to willingly accept your fingers or toothbrush in his mouth without chomping on them. Puppy teeth are needle-sharp, and even when he outgrows them, you don't want your fingers in the mouth of an uncooperative adult Boxer.

How to Brush Your Boxer's Teeth

If he's never had his teeth brushed, acquaint him with the process.

- Gently stroke the outside of one of his cheeks with your finger.

- Once he's comfortable with that, dab some dog toothpaste (never human toothpaste; it's not intended for consumption by man or beast) on your finger and allow him to taste it. Dog toothpastes come in flavors like chicken, peanut butter, and cheese—all the tastes dogs love.

- At this point, move on to a real toothbrush or a dental finger sheath with a textured

Establishing a dental care regimen with your Boxer from the time he is young is crucial to keeping his teeth clean and healthy.

Hyperplasia

Boxer's are predisposed to an overgrowth of gum tissue, called *hyperplasia*. These growths can be localized or occur throughout the mouth. The overgrown tissues themselves are not painful or harmful, but they cause other problems. They can grow to a point where the tooth crown is buried under the overgrown tissue, and the tooth becomes useless. Overgrown tissue also forms pockets that are the perfect breeding ground for harmful bacteria that, over time, can lead to very threatening systemic blood infection. To prevent such complications, overgrowths are snipped off while the dog is under general anesthesia. Recovery is quick, with little or no discomfort or bleeding.

surface to remove plaque and massage the gums. Your finger inside the sheath acts as a toothbrush.

- Brush just a few teeth at first to accustom him to the sensation.

- Work up to brushing for 30 seconds at a time, preferably one side at a time, and taking care to reach the back molars where plaque tends to accumulate. You only need to reach the outer surfaces of the teeth; the surfaces facing inward don't typically accrue much tartar.

- Lavish praise on your Boxer when you're finished,so that he will look forward to future brushings.

With a healthy diet and regular checkups, your Boxer's teeth will look as clean as his wild ancestors' and should provide a lifetime free of dental woes.

HOW TO FIND A PROFESSIONAL GROOMER

The same care you use to find a breeder, veterinarian, or pet sitter should be used to find a dog groomer. Even though the Boxer's grooming needs are small, if you choose to have these needs tended to by someone else, it's your responsibility to find a compassionate, experienced professional.

Networking is still the best way to learn about dog professionals in your area, as a personal referral is more reliable than an advertisement in the phone book or online. Contact these sources:
- other Boxer owners you know

- your veterinarian (most practices provide grooming services)

- your breeder (if local)

- your state branch of the American Boxer Club (ABC)

- The National Dog Groomers Association of America (NDGAA)

No matter how you obtain the names of potential groomers, always ask to meet the groomer, with your dog, to see how they interact. You want to make sure that you are putting your Boxer in capable, compassionate hands in accordance with your own standards.

CHAPTER 7

BOXER NUTRITIONAL NEEDS

As anyone with an Italian, Greek, or Jewish mother can attest, some ethnicities view food in general, and their own cuisine in particular, as a demonstration of love and plenty. But overindulgence in these "love feasts" often translates into unhealthy obesity. Providing your Boxer with unlimited food is not in his best interest; you actually may be doing him a disservice. By learning about canine nutrition and digestion, an appropriate diet designed to work with his physiology can feed his body while your love and attention feed your Boxer's soul.

THE BUILDING BLOCKS OF NUTRITION

Dogs in the wild are omnivores, meaning that they meet their nutritional needs by eating both plant and animal matter. When a wild dog kills a prey animal, he consumes every part of that animal, including the stomach and its contents. The meat provides protein, the bones provide essential minerals, and the digestive tract of herbivorous prey provides the small amount of vegetable matter he needs to round out his diet.

Carbohydrates

Carbohydrates aid digestion and elimination, and include sugars, starch, and cellulose. About 5 percent of a Boxer's complete diet should be fiber from carbohydrates, which necessitates some plant consumption. Good sources of fiber include boiled potatoes, carrots, brown rice, and whole grains. Excess carbohydrates are stored in the body for later use, but it's hard to imagine an active Boxer with many carbohydrates to spare.

Fats

Fat is used as an energy source and keeps your Boxer's skin healthy and coat shiny. Eating the right balance of fats is important. Too much fat results in obesity and can lead to other health problems. Insufficient fats can cause itchy skin, a dull coat, dandruff, and even ear infections. Dietary fats help protect the short-coated Boxer from extreme cold and also make his food tasty.

Proteins

Protein is important for bone growth, tissue healing, and the daily replacement of spent body tissues. All animal tissue has a pretty high protein level, but because it isn't stored in

Dogs need a variety of nutrients in their diet, including plenty of fresh, cool water.

the body, a dog must get the protein he needs from food every day of his life. Proteins are made up of 25 "building blocks" called amino acids. Essential amino acids must be obtained from food, while nonessential amino acids are manufactured within the body.

Minerals

Minerals are nutritional elements obtained from food. *Calcium* and *phosphorus* work together to prevent rickets and other bone deformities, as well as to aid in tooth formation, muscle development, and lactation in nursing bitches. *Potassium* contributes to normal growth and healthy nerves and muscles, while *sodium* and *chlorine* maintain appetite and normal activity levels. *Magnesium* helps synthesize proteins and prevents nervous system problems. *Iron* is important for healthy blood, aided by *copper*. *Iodine* prevents goiter (enlarged thyroid), while *zinc* promotes healthy skin. *Cobalt* promotes normal growth and a sound reproductive tract, aided by *manganese*. As with vitamins, supplement minerals only under your veterinarian's advice.

Vitamins

Vitamins are organic compounds that function as metabolic regulators in the body. A balanced diet should provide all of the vitamins your Boxer needs. Supplements should be given only under vet supervision, as it's easy to overdose and create health problems where none existed.

Vitamin A is used for fat absorption, and promotes good eyesight, normal growth rate,

By the Numbers

A simple formula to determine how many calories a healthy adult Boxer should ingest daily is 30 calories per 1 pound (.5 kg) of desired weight. A 50-pound (22.5 kg) Boxer's daily caloric intake is about 1,500. The number may increase or decrease depending on size, activity level, and age.

and reproduction. *B vitamins* are important for coat, skin, appetite, growth, and eyes. They also protect the nervous system and aid metabolism. *Vitamin C* is synthesized in a dog's liver, so it's not usually added to a dog's diet. Same goes for *vitamin K*, which is synthesized in the digestive tract. *Vitamin D* is essential for healthy bones, teeth, and muscle tone, but must be taken with the proper ratio of calcium and phosphorus. *Vitamin E* promotes proper muscle function, internal and reproductive organs, and all cell membrane function.

Water
Proper hydration has enjoyed a new popularity; everyone you see carries a bottle of water. Your Boxer doesn't need trendy spring water, but he does need lots of cool, fresh water to drink throughout the day, every day. A healthy dog should consume, from food and drink, 1/2 to 3/4 fluid ounces (15 to 20 mL) per 1 pound (0.5 kg) of body weight per day. In hot weather and after exercise, he'll need more. Excessive thirst can also be a symptom of illness, so check with your vet if you notice more drinking than usual.

WHAT TO FEED
Commercial dog food options these days extend far beyond the old days of canned horse meat, once a popular choice. Fortunately, dog food companies have made strides in improving the quality of their products, and people are better equipped

A balanced diet will keep your Boxer looking and feeling his best.

today to make educated decisions about a healthy canine diet.

Commercial Dog Foods

Commercial dog food is still the most popular way to feed your dog, and dozens of products are available to prove it. In relatively recent years, dog food companies have recognized the special dietary needs of different life stages. Foods are now formulated especially for puppies, healthy adult dogs, overweight dogs, and senior citizens. There are also formulas acceptable for all stages of life, labeled as "100 percent nutritionally complete." However, further food choices can be made within this food type.

Dry Food (Kibble)

Dry dog food is a popular and economical commercial food choice. Dry food keeps well without refrigeration and may be bought in bulk quantities. The chewing action of crunchy dry food also helps reduce tartar buildup on your dog's teeth. Read the package labels carefully. Ingredients are listed in order of predominance, from greatest to least. Choose a brand that uses a wholesome digestible protein as its primary ingredient—that is, one of the first four listed.

Semi-Moist Food

Semi-moist foods are shaped like chops, burgers, or other meaty-looking facsimiles. But don't be fooled: they are usually the least wholesome of all commercial dog foods, filled with artificial coloring, flavors, and scents. They don't fit the nutritional bill as an exclusive diet but can be used as tasty occasional treats.

Canned Food (Wet)

Canned, or wet, dog food smells and tastes great to a dog, and its long shelf life makes it easy and convenient. It can also be costly, and the soft consistency does little for a dog's oral hygiene. It's easy to find at supermarkets and convenience stores, but how much *digestible* protein is it really providing? Read the labels for nutritional information. How much "filler" (processed grain and/or animal by-products) is added?

Whichever type of commercial food you prefer, opt for a well-balanced, high-quality brand that meets your dog's nutritional needs. Some excellent dry foods on the market use quality ingredients with very little or no filler, although they are not always conveniently sold at supermarkets. You may have to make an extra trip to a specialty store to find them, but isn't your Boxer worth the effort?

Noncommercial Foods

Dog owners are becoming increasingly discerning about pet nutrition, many

Training Tidbit

Food is an effective training tool, but you should never deprive your Boxer of food for training purposes. Survival instincts overrule a dog's desire to please his human, and a hungry dog will do whatever it takes to obtain food. Aside from the fact that you owe your dog the security and basic health of regular, quality food, you want him to learn the positive rewards of obedience.

Feeding DO's and DON'T's

The DO'S of Feeding Your Boxer

- DO make sure that your Boxer's food is tasty for him, or he won't eat it!
- DO read nutrition labels of commercial dog foods, and choose a good-quality, nutrient-balanced food.
- DO look for natural preservatives like vitamin E or food without preservatives at all.
- DO be consistent with the kind of food you choose, as long as it is satisfactory. A sudden change in diet can upset your dog's digestive system, so refrain from jumping from brand to brand.
- DO ensure that fresh, clean, cool water is available at all times.

The DON'T's of Feeding Your Boxer

- DON'T use foods with chemical preservatives like BHT and ethoxyquin, which are suspected carcinogens.
- DON'T overfeed. Your breeder and/or veterinarian can advise you on the proper amounts and frequency of meals. Don't count on your APBT to stop eating when he's full!
- DON'T feed table scraps. Dogs' bodies are not constructed like ours and therefore do not have the same nutritional needs or food processing capabilities that we do. Some common foods, such as chocolate and onions, are toxic to dogs.
- DON'T give your Boxer small meat bones (other than cooked beef knucklebones) because they can splinter and cause serious injury to your dog's digestive tract.
- DON'T overdo doggie treats. They should supplement your dog's diet, not replace it.

preferring to feed a diet as close as possible to that which Mother Nature intended, without preservatives and chemical additives, or even without cooking at all. Noncommercial dog foods may require more education and effort than opening a can or bag of commercial food, but the vitality rewards amply compensate.

The Home-Cooked Diet

Some Boxer owners prefer to be in complete control of their dogs' nutrition. Properly researched and prepared, a homemade diet is an excellent way to make sure that your dog is eating right.

Make no mistake: The home-cooked diet is not simply can-opening or pouch-tearing. It requires considerable education and experience to be sure that you're feeding your Boxer what he needs. Preparation is time-consuming and more costly than buying commercially prepared dog food. In fact, the number of people who feed only home-cooked food to their dogs has dwindled in the last 20 years due to the improvement in quality commercial foods. If you feel that

Properly researched, a homemade diet is an excellent way to insure your Boxer is eating well.

your Boxer will benefit from a homemade diet, become an expert in canine nutrition and consult with your vet. The last thing you want is to unintentionally deprive him of the proper nutrients.

The BARF (Biologically Appropriate Raw Food) Diet

It's sometimes hard to remember that the Boxer companion sprawled on your lap is descended from a wolf who ate a variety of plant matter consumed by his prey. Dogs have very short intestinal tracts and strong stomach acids that are geared toward consuming and digesting raw food. Despite thousands of years of domestication, their digestive system has remained pretty much the same. Why not feed them the diet for which their bodies are designed?

Ideally, a raw diet includes bones and organs in addition to meat. Remember, our dogs' wild ancestors consumed the entire prey, not just the flesh. But what about small bones of animals like chicken which, as we've always been warned, can splinter? The fact is that cooked chicken bones can splinter, but raw bones crunch into small pieces that clean the teeth and gums. Bones are also a natural source of calcium and phosphorus.

There are a few precautions you should take when feeding a raw diet. Some are obvious, like washing your hands after handling raw meat to fight bacteria and thawing frozen meat in the refrigerator instead of at room temperature to prevent bacteria growth. Don't microwave raw food, even as briefly as 30 seconds, as this will damage the live enzymes and harden the bones. Although we are told that eating raw or undercooked meat can be risky, the chance of a dog contracting parasites from properly handled raw meat is much less than from wild prey. It's wise, however, to avoid raw pork, which can transmit trichinella, a parasite historically found iin undercooked pork. As with any new diet, introduce it slowly to your Boxer. Incorporate it into his current diet in stages, gradually decreasing the proportion of his accustomed food and increasing the raw food.

BARF diets have been common practice in Europe for years, particularly in Germany. Fear of bacteria and parasites initially kept the United States from embracing this routine but the risk now seems to have been put into perspective. Not only is the dog's physiology designed to accommodate the diet, more nutrients are available in fresh, raw food. Teeth are kept clean and white, coats are healthier, and the immune system is bolstered. Educational websites and online stores make buying the right foods easy.

There are no magic cures for medical ailments, but many BARF-feeding Boxer owners swear that the return to their dogs' evolutionary roots has relieved their pets of allergies and other skin conditions, cleared up gastrointestinal and chronic ear problems, and maintained clean teeth and breath. It requires more planning and work than pouring kibble into a dish, but the payoff is worthwhile. Check with your vet to see if this option is right for your Boxer.

Special Diets

Sometimes even a healthy dog is better served by a customized diet because of specific physical conditions, such as atypically small or large size, daily activity level, or individual metabolism.

Prescription Foods

A Boxer may develop urinary problems if his food has high mineral levels. Even protein can be provided in excess, contributing to urinary stones, a painful and potentially serious condition. Regular checkups that include urinalysis will easily detect if the urine is forming crystals, a precursor to stones. Your vet may recommend a prescription food that

Multi-Dog Tip

Food aggression can occur if one or more dogs in a multi-dog home become possessive about their food. One dog may growl or snap at a "sibling" who comes near the feeding area, even if the dog has no interest in the food itself. Feeding all family dogs at the same time should eliminate jealousy or anxiety, but if the alpha dog in your pack acts on his ancient instincts to garner the lion's share for himself, you may need to separate dogs at feeding time. Something as simple as moving food bowls to opposite ends of the same area may be all you need to do. In cases of ongoing food aggression, though, separate "dining rooms" may be warranted, such as placing each dog inside his respective crate. In severe cases, you may need to seek professional help.

Even dogs who get along well may become food possessive.

carefully balances those nutrients known to cause problems.

Dogs with sensitive stomachs or with an allergy to certain foods may also require a customized diet, such as lamb and rice formula. Treats may need to be limited to specific ingredients. Your vet will advise you on the best protocol to follow.

Commercially prepared and packaged prescription foods are available through veterinarians and on the Internet. As with any product you buy online for convenience or lower prices—especially health-related products—quality control is an issue. You must be confident in the integrity of the seller lest you unwittingly buy an unregulated, lesser-quality product intentionally advertised and sold as an established brand.

Supplements

A wholesome diet should provide all of the nutrients your Boxer needs, but there are times in a dog's life when food supplementation is beneficial. A pregnant or nursing female needs a little more food than she normally eats. A show dog who is frequently on the road may experience more stress than a "civilian" dog and need more nutrition. A dog with joint problems may benefit from supplements thought to encourage cartilage growth. If you feel that your Boxer would benefit from extra food or nutritional supplements, consult your vet first. Supplements are easily overdosed and can lead to a variety of ailments.

OBESITY

An overweight Boxer is an unhealthy dog, period. Obesity adds stress to his joints and forces his internal organs to work harder. At some point during the aging process, your Boxer's metabolism will slow down. If you don't reduce the amount of calories accordingly, he'll gain unneeded weight. Saying no to extra treats and "junk food" snacks isn't harsh; you're demonstrating your love by keeping your Boxer's weight at an appropriate level. Regular exercise will help a healthy adult keep his beautiful physique.

WHEN TO FEED AN ADULT BOXER

A typical adult Boxer eats two meals a day, the equivalent of breakfast and dinner, with the amount adjusted according to his specific nutritional needs. Even dogs with the same lifestyles can have slightly different metabolisms that require more or less food.

Want to Know More?

For more information on how to use treats as training rewards, see Chapter 9: Boxer Training.

Some dogs eat more in winter than in summer. An older school of thought recommended one meal a day for adult dogs, but it makes more metabolic sense to divide the portion into two meals that will provide steady fuel throughout the day.

Under professional guidance, you can experiment until you find the right type, amount, and frequency of food that best suit your Boxer. Changes in food must be done gradually to avoid upsetting his stomach. Adding a little of a new food to his regular food, in increasing amounts over a week or so, won't be a shock to his system. Once you've found the food he likes best and that provides the best nutrition, his bright eyes, shiny coat, healthy musculature, and happy disposition will tell the tale.

CHAPTER 8

BOXER HEALTH AND WELLNESS

All the tender loving care in the world isn't always enough to keep your Boxer in good health. Regular exercise, wholesome food, fresh water, and frequent brushing go a long way toward his well-being, but regular preventive veterinary care is a crucial component in the formula.

THE ANNUAL VET EXAM

Regular physical examinations begin with his first puppy checkup once you bring your Boxer home, no later than three days from the time he becomes a family member. Not only can the vet make sure that your puppy is in good physical shape, but she can acquaint herself with the dog in a minimally invasive situation. A dog who associates trips to the vet with unpleasantness may become anxious about future visits, and you don't want regular checkups to be traumatic ordeals for your Boxer or you. Remember that dogs are keenly sensitive to our moods and feelings. If you display any anxiety about veterinary exams or procedures, your Boxer will detect the tension. If he wasn't nervous himself, he'll regard your apprehension as a reason to get nervous! If you like and trust your veterinarian, your Boxer will, too.

What Happens at an Annual Exam

Regular veterinary examinations are your adult Boxer's best defense against health problems, mild or serious. Knowing what to expect at well-dog checkups will help you identify potential symptoms in the future, in addition to maintaining a calm demeanor during exams. Hold your Boxer gently but firmly during the vet's examination, talking to him in a happy, upbeat tone. Unfortunately, our human instinct to comfort and soothe is counterintuitive when applied to a dog. If you coddle him with too much hugging or consoling, he'll get the idea that something bad is about to happen.

Nose

The vet will check your Boxer's nose for any abnormal discharge, not whether it's cold and wet. Contrary to folklore that proclaims that a healthy dog's nose is always cold and wet, your Boxer can be in perfect health and have a dry nose for no other reason than his tongue can't reach that high. If the exterior appears chapped or scratched, the vet may suggest a topical ointment.

Regular vet exams are your Boxer's best defense against health problems.

Eyes

Boxers have very expressive eyes that should be bright and alert when the dog is happy and healthy. Dull, lifeless eyes are often the first indication that something is amiss, whether it's emotional stress, internal parasites, or a serious illness. The vet will check the eyes for any debris or abnormal (bloody, yellow, green) discharge that may indicate a contagious eye infection. The clear or whitish mucus that Boxers' eyes often secrete is normal, unless it's in copious amounts. The vet will check for any cloudiness in the eyes that could indicate corneal ulcerations or cataracts, which usually afflict older dogs. She will also look for any redness of the eye, indicating a possible irritant. If your Boxer's haws (the nictitating membrane or third eyelid) are white (transparent), they may reveal a redness that looks like an irritation although the eye is perfectly normal.

Mouth

The vet will look inside your Boxer's mouth for any lumps, cuts, or scrapes to the soft tissue that may indicate a tooth abscess, tumor, or allergic reaction to an insect bite. She will also check the color of his gums, which should be a deep pink. (Pale pink gums can indicate dehydration.) Healthy teeth will appear clean and white. Healthy puppies typically experience no mouth problems, but annual exams as he ages will include checking for plaque accumulation on teeth that can lead to gingivitis (gum disease), as well as gingival hyperplasia, an overgrowth of gum tissue frequently noted in Boxers. The tumors are not harmful in themselves but provide a hospitable environment for bacterial proliferation and subsequent infection. In extreme cases, the excess tissue can interfere with the dog's bite.

Ears

The vet will examine your Boxer's ears with an otoscope, a handheld, lighted instrument that affords a view inside the ear. The dark, moist, warm environment inside the ear is a friendly harbor for bacteria. A discharge, foul odor, or inflammation in the ear may signify infection. She will also check for ear mites, highly transmittable parasites that can make your Boxer miserable.

An old wives' tale once claimed that cropped ears are less likely to develop ear infections and other troubles, but that is false. A new Boxer owner should not visit on her puppy a procedure like ear cropping under the misconception that it is in her dog's best interest.

Lungs

The vet will use a stethoscope to listen to your Boxer's lungs for any congestion or abnormal breathing patterns. Chest congestion can be a symptom of diseases like bordetella (kennel cough), distemper, and even heartworm.

Heart

A dog's normal heart rate ranges from 100 to 130 beats per minute. Any variation from that range warrants concern, especially because cardiomyopathy and other heart diseases are commonly found in Boxers. Early detection of any cardiac arrhythmia is your dog's best chance for a greater life expectancy.

Skin and Coat

The skin is the largest organ in the body and reveals much about a dog's overall state of health. The vet will check for fleas, ticks, and other external parasites. Flea "dirt" (excrement) can appear as tiny specks of

At his annual vet visit, the vet will examine your Boxer's ears and eyes.

A dog with internal parasites will show signs of general malaise.

black pepper on the skin, also indicating flea infestation. The vet will also look for any swellings, scratches, scaly patches, and any lumps under the skin. A healthy coat will appear shiny and even.

Abdomen

The vet will palpate your Boxer's abdomen for lumps, abnormal distention, or possible infections. She'll pay attention to any signs of pain from the dog during palpation, another indicator of trouble.

Back and Tail

The vet will visually and manually inspect the dog's spine and tail for any abnormalities that may indicate problems like intervertebral disk disease (IVD), in

which the gelatinous cushioning substance inside each spinal disk protrudes, placing pressure on the spinal column and causing acute pain. This affliction is more often seen in breeds with disproportionately short legs, such as Dachshunds, Corgis, and Bulldogs, but can affect Boxers.

Boxers' tails are typically docked short soon after they're born, thereby reducing the risk of injury or infection. If your Boxer's tail has not been docked (there is no medical need to do so; it is strictly cosmetic), the vet will check it for any topical abnormalities or possible breakage.

Paws

The vet will check the paw pads for any lacerations, punctures, or swellings. She will also check between the toes, a common breeding ground for yeast infection. If nails need to be trimmed, a veterinary assistant can take care of that now.

PARASITES

A parasite is an organism that exploits other organisms for its own existence, without benefitting the "host" organism. Parasites fall into two groups: ectoparasites, which live on the outside, and endoparasites, which live on the inside of the body. Both can be the bane of your Boxer's existence if not treated. They can make him uncomfortable, sick, and downright miserable. In the extreme, such as with heartworms, they can kill.

As humans have discovered over the last few hundred years, good grooming, hygienic practices, and clean living conditions help protect against parasites. Modern veterinary medicine has also developed an array of preventive treatments that effectively reduce our dogs' risk of parasite infestation. There are also natural prophylactics against parasites to satisfy the dog owner wishing to eschew chemical insecticides, although their efficacy and reliability cannot be confirmed. Discuss with your vet which parasites you need to beware and what treatments are best suited to your Boxer.

Want to Know More?

For information on diseases that veterinarians commonly vaccinate against, see Chapter 3: Care of Your Boxer.

Internal Parasites

In addition to vaccinating against contagious diseases, your vet will perform a yearly check for internal parasites like heartworms and several kinds of intestinal worms.

Conscientious breeders see that their litters receive the necessary treatment for intestinal worms, a common affliction of puppies. Many pups are born with roundworms, and those who aren't can easily become infested. A puppy should be worm-free by the time he goes to his new home, but that doesn't guarantee against future worm infestations. A dog with intestinal worms will show signs of general malaise: a dry coat, dull eyes, weakness, coughing and vomiting, diarrhea, and/or weight loss despite a hearty appetite. Some dogs, though, will lose their appetite entirely, and still others are asymptomatic until worm infestation renders them severely anemic.

Heartworms

Heartworms are deadly parasites transmitted from dog to dog through mosquito bites. The heartworm-infested mosquito bites the dog and deposits heartworm larvae into his skin. The larvae then enter the dog's system through the hole made by the bite and establish residence in the blood vessels. It can be a full eight months after the bite before the worms mature. As they start to interfere with heart function, symptoms will appear: a chronic cough, weight loss, and fatigue. Heart failure ultimately claims the dog's life.

An infestation of adult heartworms is treatable, but treatment is expensive, long, and risky, although not as dangerous as the heartworms themselves. The process kills the adult heartworms, but dead worms in the heart can provoke a fatal clot in the blood

You are your dog's best advocate when it comes to his health.

vessels or chambers. Prevention is a far better way to spare your Boxer a premature death from this disease. Your vet can tell you the right age to start your dog on a heartworm preventive and which ones she recommends. A monthly dose of the medicine, usually in the form of a meaty morsel or flavored tablet, is all it takes to guard against heartworms throughout your dog's lifetime.

There is a caveat, however. Your dog must be tested and found free of heartworms before starting a preventive regimen. A dog already harboring heartworms can become critically ill from the same medicine that prevents infestation. Heartworm prevention isn't foolproof, and there is always a slight chance that a dog on a prophylactic regimen can become infested. Because the symptoms

don't present themselves for many months, you could innocently make your infected dog sick by continuing his heartworm preventive. It is therefore important to have your Boxer's blood tested once a year for the presence of heartworms.

Hookworms

Dog owners in the United States need to be concerned with four different species of this blood-sucking worm, of which the most common and most serious are found in warm climates. One variety prefers colder climates, thereby posing a concern for dog owners in the northern US and Canada. Hookworms can cause severe iron-deficiency anemia in dogs, and create a problem for humans, too, although hookworms cannot complete their life cycle in a human host. They simply infest human skin and cause irritation. Transmission is through infected feces, so using proper implements and/or disposable gloves when cleaning up waste is a good way to prevent hookworm infestation.

In canine hosts, hookworms attach themselves to the intestines to feed, changing locations about six times a day. The dog loses blood each time the hookworm repositions itself and can become anemic. Symptoms of hookworm infestation include dark stools, weight loss, general weakness, pale skin coloration, and skin problems. Luckily, a number of proven medications are available to rid the host of these parasites. Most heartworm preventives conveniently include a hookworm insecticide.

Ringworm

Ringworm is not really a worm but a very contagious fungus that spreads easily among animals and humans through contact with infected skin or hair. Infective spores are constantly dropped from the hair and skin of infected dogs or people, and contact with even one spore is all it takes to become contaminated. The ringworm fungus feeds on the dead surface skin and hair cells, causing an irritating itch. It typically appears on dogs as a raw-looking bald patch that will sometimes appear scaly, without the rawness.

As with many fungal infections, ringworm is difficult to eliminate. It's very hardy in the environment and can live for years. It can resist treatment, which includes a combination of topical and systemic medication therapy. Painstaking attention to hygiene and complete decontamination of the dog's environment must be continued

Plenty of exercise will help keep your Boxer healthy and feeling his best.

until the vet declares the dog ringworm-free. Children, the elderly, and adults with compromised immune systems are most susceptible. If your dog is diagnosed with ringworm and you don't have it at that time, chances are you won't contract it.

Roundworms

Roundworms are very common parasites in puppies and adult dogs. Even puppies from responsible breeders often have them. If the mother dog ever had roundworms, she may have larvae encysted in her body that she can pass on through her milk, even if an examination revealed no intestinal infestation. Puppies in utero can be infested when the mother's worm cysts migrate to their developing lungs during pregnancy. Every puppy in the litter will most likely be born with roundworms and require several treatments. Dogs and humans can also pick up roundworm from the ground, where the eggs have been deposited by other animals, including beetles, earthworms, and rodents.

Roundworms look like strands of spaghetti and can be up to 8 inches (20.5 cm) long. Like the tapeworm, they feed off the host's digesting food. Infested puppies at first will eat voraciously but quickly weaken from malnutrition and stop eating altogether. A pup with an acute or chronic roundworm infestation will develop a "pot belly" (noticeably larger than the normal "puppy belly"), diarrhea, and vomiting. The condition is easily treated, but humans in the family who have had contact with a puppy suffering from roundworms need to be especially vigilant about their own hygiene.

Tapeworms

The tapeworm is actually a parasite of a parasite. It enters a dog's system when a dog

Multi-Dog Tip

Here are three good reasons to immediately collect and dispose of stools if you have multiple dogs (and even if you have just one dog):
1. Enables you to perform a handy visual check on your Boxer's digestive health. Blood, diarrhea, black-colored or dark stools may all indicate potential health problems.
2. Avoids spreading disease and/or parasites you're unaware of yet.
3. Prevents coprophagia (eating of feces, either the dog's own or another animal's).

eats fleas infested with tapeworm larvae. The larvae move into the intestines, where they develop into adults, sometimes growing to be several feet (m) long. Adult tapeworms feed on the host's digesting food, robbing him of nutrition. Humans infested with tapeworms are constantly hungry and eat ravenously but don't gain weight. Extreme cases can be fatal.

Tapeworms don't always appear in a dog's stool but are diagnosed when small segments appear around the anus. These are parts of the worm that break off and stick to the hair and tissue around the anus, resembling wriggling grains of rice. They tickle the anus and the dog may scoot his behind along the floor to relieve it. If you see any worms in his feces, or if he scoots along the floor, take him to the vet. The condition is easily treated, but you also need to address the issue of fleas because they are the most common carriers.

Whipworms

In North America, whipworms are among the most common parasitic worms in dogs, attaching themselves to the lower part of the intestine to feed. They can live for months or even years in a host dog, spending the larval stage in the small intestine, the adult stage in the large intestine, and passing eggs through the dog's feces.

The affected dog may only have an upset stomach and some diarrhea, making whipworms hard to diagnose. Left untreated, anemia can develop. The only way to detect whipworms is with a stool sample examination, and even this is not infallible. Dogs successfully treated for whipworms are often reinfected from exposure to the eggs deposited on the ground in feces. Whipworm eggs can survive in the environment as long as five years, waiting to infest—or reinfest—a host, thus emphasizing the importance of proper waste removal, whether in your own backyard or a public park.

External Parasites

Fleas, ticks, ear mites, and mange mites all think that your Boxer would make the perfect host, but such guests will only make him uncomfortable and potentially sick. They can be found anywhere on his body but typically settle on the head and neck. External parasite prevention often means introducing insecticides into your dog's body, the long-term effects of which concern many dog owners. There is no documentation that long-term pesticide use poses health risks, but there is plenty of information on parasite-borne diseases. Talk to your vet about the best course of action for the well-being of your Boxer.

Fleas

Fleas are common, bloodsucking parasites that have long afflicted humans as well as dogs and are by far the hardest external parasite to eradicate. Their bite causes chronic discomfort and can transmit myriad diseases, not the least of which includes bubonic plague. Not only do they reproduce incredibly fast, they can actually adapt and become resistant to insecticides. They can quickly invade your home, laying eggs in carpets, bedding, and furniture. Other than telltale scratching, how do you know if your Boxer is bothered by fleas? With your fingers, separate a patch of his fur to examine his skin. If you see tiny black flecks that look like pepper, that's flea "dirt," or excrement. Some dogs develop serious allergic reactions to flea bites.

To control a flea infestation, adult fleas must be killed before they have a chance to reproduce. Your vet can recommend a course of action that may include bathing your Boxer with an insecticidal additive, usually done at the vet's. Topical flea-killing treatments are available commercially, but consult your vet before applying any pesticide. The vet can also provide guidance

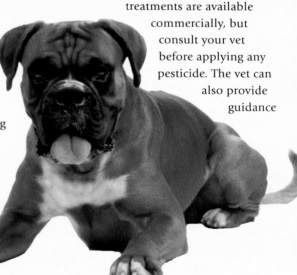

Check your dog for fleas and ticks after he's been playing outdoors.

on the steps necessary to rid your living environment of fleas, inside and outside. Sometimes a pest control company may be needed to help overcome these unwelcome guests. Diligence in all areas is paramount to the successful annihilation of fleas.

Prevention is the best solution to fleas, and many products, chemical and organic, are commercially available to help, ranging from pesticide-infused collars to herbal tinctures. Consult your vet to find the best flea-prevention protocol for your Boxer.

Mites

Mites are tiny arachnids, various types of which are parasitic. Ear mites live in the ear canal, irritating your Boxer's sensitive ears and producing a dry, rusty-brown discharge. If you see your dog constantly scratching or pawing at his ears or notice inflammation or

discharge, have your vet check for ear mites.

Mange mites are tiny parasites that can cause big dermatological problems for your Boxer. They can cause sarcoptic mange, making his skin itchy and crusty and raising little red bumps; and demodectic or red mange, a red, hairless condition caused by demodex mites that live in the hair follicles and sebaceous glands. Mange is a problem that should not be allowed to progress. Your vet can recommend the best course of action to rid your Boxer of the nasty creatures that cause it.

Ticks

Like mites, ticks are arachnids that feed off their host's blood by burrowing their mouths into the skin. They typically wait in outdoor vegetation until a potential host, such as a dog, passes by. The tick can drop from a tree or bush onto the dog's head and shoulder area or hop aboard one of his legs or paws. More than just a nuisance, ticks can carry disease. The tiny deer tick—no bigger than a poppy seed—is especially known to carry Lyme disease, a flu-like illness causing fatigue, fever, loss of appetite, and swollen neck glands. Humans are susceptible to Lyme disease and need to guard against tick bites. Ticks are also bearers of Rocky Mountain spotted fever, which can cause paralysis in dogs. Even ticks not carrying disease are hazardous to dogs who are allergic to the tick's saliva. Adverse reactions can develop, ranging from swelling to paralysis. Tick-bite sites can become infected and develop into a serious secondary bacterial illness.

Ticks come in many sizes and colors, from brown to almost blue, and are fairly easy to spot on the Boxer's short coat. Ticks must never be allowed to remain on a dog or a human but should be removed carefully. Old-fashioned removal methods such as holding a hot match tip to the tick or piercing it with a needle are not advisable. A hot match or cigarette not only risks burning the dog but causes the tick to embed more deeply. A needle risks piercing the dog's skin and potentially spreading disease by exposing the tick's body fluid. The simplest, safest, and most popular method of tick removal has been to pull it out with a pair of blunt tweezers that you dedicated for that purpose. Grasp the tick as close to its head as possible, pull it out with a steady movement, and flush it down the toilet. Try not to rupture or squeeze the tick's body; you don't want potentially infectious body fluids to get on the dog's skin or your hand. Don't leave the head in, which can become infected. If part of the tick's head does remain attached, apply an antiseptic to the site to prevent infection. It will eventually fall off in a few days. It may be a good idea to visit the vet to be sure that infection has not occurred.

Many dog owners swear by safe, easy tick removal methods that are much easier on dog and human. One way is to separate the dog's fur at the tick site and rub the tick's body with your finger in a circular motion for about a minute. The tick will retract its head from under the skin, making it easy for you to pick off the intact tick. Another method advocates squeezing a dollop of dishwashing liquid onto a cotton ball and applying it to the tick site. The soap will cause the tick to retract its head, enabling you to simply pick up the whole parasite with the cotton ball.

BOXER-SPECIFIC HEALTH ISSUES

Although most ailments can affect any dog of any breed, some are more prevalent in certain breeds than others. This does not imply that all Boxers will develop illnesses common in the breed or that all Boxers will develop only those illnesses. Familiarity with these health issues, though, can facilitate early diagnosis and successful treatment.

By the Numbers

Certain physical problems develop with age, as any grandparent can attest. A Boxer is considered a senior at seven years, so yearly veterinary examinations become even more important to his continued good health.

Brachycephalic Disorders

Along with breeds like the Bulldog, Pekingese, and Pug, Boxers are brachycephalic, meaning "short, broad headed." Their very short muzzles often indicate anomalies in the upper respiratory tract and greater susceptibility to conditions like heatstroke. Irony lies in the fact that the same short muzzles that promote brachycephalic disorders in Boxers once enabled the baiting Boxer to breathe more freely while performing his gruesome tasks.

Brachycephalic Airway Obstruction Syndrome

All brachycephalic breeds experience brachycephalic airway obstruction syndrome (BAOS) to some degree, including Boxers. Examples of very pronounced BAOS are seen in Bulldogs, Pekingese, and Cavalier King Charles Spaniels. Some breed standards specify very short facial dimensions that leave little space for normal-sized breathing structures. Thus, ideal conformation breeding can perpetuate the syndrome's inheritance. Repercussions of BAOS can range from snoring to respiratory collapse.

Stenotic Nares

A component of BAOS, stenotic nares are pinched nostrils often seen in brachycephalic breeds. They are an inherited trait and can make breathing difficult. In extreme cases, veterinarians can perform a simple surgical procedure to widen the nostrils and ease breathing. If your Boxer habitually snorts and snores heavily, you may wish to consult your vet about corrective options.

Gastric Torsion (Bloat)

Gastric torsion, or bloat, is a serious health concern in which a dog's stomach swells and twists from excess gas, water, or both. Imagine the bloated stomach as a Tootsie Roll with the ends of the wrapper twisted tightly. When torsion occurs, the esophagus is closed off, limiting the dog's ability to relieve distention by vomiting or belching. Often the spleen becomes entrapped as well, and its blood supply is obstructed. A chain of deadly physiological events begins that culminates in shock and heart failure. An otherwise healthy dog can die a painful death from gastric torsion in a matter of hours. Quick treatment is crucial to saving his life.

Although some dogs may have a genetic predisposition to it, bloat is suspected to be the result of certain external factors:

- strenuous exercise after a large meal and/or large water intake
- mealtime agitation and stress

Eating only one meal per day could contribute to your dog contracting bloat.

Boxers are prone to breathing problems because they have very short facial dimensions.

- gender and age (males and dogs over two years of age seem to be more often afflicted)
- eating too fast
- eating only one meal per day

You'll know if your Boxer is experiencing gastric torsion by its dramatic symptoms:
- obvious abdominal pain and swelling
- excessive drooling and panting
- dazed, "shocky" look
- repeated attempts to vomit
- pale, cool-to-the-touch skin in and around the mouth

If you see any of these signs in your dog, seek immediate help and don't panic. Call ahead so that the vet can prepare for your arrival. They will first try to decompress the stomach with a stomach tube. Often this takes care of the situation, but if it doesn't, immediate surgery is required to correct the twisted stomach, remove unhealthy tissue, and anchor the stomach in place to avoid recurrences of bloat.

The stomach-anchoring procedure, called gastropexy, is performed prophylactically on dogs whose previous bouts of distension predispose them to future bouts or who have close relatives who were victims of bloat. Gastropexy is a drastic measure that should be considered only if other preventive efforts have failed. Simple changes like increasing the frequency of your dog's meals, refraining from strenuous exercise right after meals, and not allowing him to drink large amounts of water right after exercise are other possible ways to prevent this dangerous condition.

Gingival Hyperplasia

Gingival hyperplasia is an overgrowth of gum tissue that presents as tumors or flaps of tissue along the gum line adjacent to the teeth. Although not life threatening themselves, these overgrowths trap food, hair, and bacteria in the mouth, which is difficult to clean and can lead to infection. If an infection becomes systemic, serious illness or even death can occur. Boxers have a propensity toward growths and tumors of all types, so this oral condition is often seen in older Boxers. Surgical excision of these growths is performed under anesthesia, at which time the vet may also recommend a full dental cleaning. Recurrence is not unlikely.

Heatstroke

Dogs typically lower their body temperature by panting, and longer-nosed breeds do this more effectively than short-nosed breeds. Moreover, the Boxer's playful and stoic nature prompt him to continue running and playing despite intense heat. Many veterinarians say that by the time a Boxer exhibits signs of overheating, the problem is already serious.

Heatstroke, or hyperthermia, occurs when body temperature is elevated due to environmental factors. This is not the same as a fever, which is a physiological increase in set body temperature. A dog is considered hyperthermic when his body temperature measures above 105°F (40.6°C). (Normal body temperature for dogs is around 101°F [38.3°C].) Heatstroke symptoms include rapid panting, weakness, disorientation, fatigue, and dark-red to purple gums. If you think that your Boxer is hyperthermic, remove him immediately to a shady area and soak him with cool water. Cold water is counterproductive because it causes the blood vessels to constrict, thus decreasing blood flow and actually retaining body heat. Transport him immediately to the veterinarian.

The best prevention against heatstroke is to limit your Boxer's activity in high temperatures. Available shade and plenty of fresh, cool drinking water are mandatory for any Boxer outdoors in summer weather, but these are not enough to prevent hyperthermia, even in the Boxer who is minimally active. Most importantly, never leave a dog in a car outdoors, even in balmy ambient temperatures. The interior of a car, even with open windows, can rise to a dangerous level within minutes and subject your Boxer to a miserable death by heatstroke. If you cannot take him into air-conditioning with you, leave him at home.

To prevent your Boxer from getting heatstroke, provide him with shade while outdoors, as well as plenty of cool drinking water. Restrict his time outdoors during intense heat and humidity.

Hip Dysplasia

This debilitating condition occurs when a malformed hip joint doesn't offer a sufficiently wide socket into which the head of the femur (thighbone) must fit. The femur can slide in and out of the socket, causing severe pain to the dog. It is considered a congenital condition, although environmental factors can contribute to its progression. It almost always appears before the dog is 18 months old, but some dogs with the condition never exhibit symptoms. This is a problem for responsible breeders who don't want to inadvertently perpetuate such a legacy. When obtaining a Boxer from a reputable breeder, always look for one whose parents were screened for hip dysplasia by the Orthopedic Foundation for Animals (OFA).

Von Willebrand's Disease

Von Willebrand's disease (vWD) is a genetic bleeding disorder sometimes seen in Boxers. It's characterized by excessive bleeding, first noticed during procedures like dew claw removals or ear croppings, and it can be life threatening in its severest form.

In dogs, there are three types: vWD I, vWD II, and vWD III. Type III, the most severe and with a high mortality rate, is most often seen in Scottish Terriers. Type I is the most common.

Blood tests can tell the range of genetic tendency toward the disease. Some dogs m

Boxers can be prone to a variety of diseases, including congenital heart disease.

ay be carriers without suffering from the disease itself, so testing of all dogs used for breeding is essential. Puppies as young as seven weeks can also be tested for the presence of vWD.

Congenital Heart Disease

Responsible breeders will have their Boxers checked for heart problems—congenital or otherwise—prior to breeding.

Valvular Disease

The heart contains four valves: the mitral valve (left AV), tricuspid valve (right AV), aortic or left semilunar valve, and the pulmonic or right semilunar valve. The most common indication of valve trouble is a heart murmur, a particular sound made by the dysfunctional valves and heard with a stethoscope.

Valvular dysfunction is either congenital or acquired. Types of valvular disease include endocarditis, a bacterial infection that affects young to middle-aged, large-breed dogs with no history of heart disease; congenital aortic stenosis, a narrowing of the outflow channel between the left ventricle and the main artery of the body (the aorta); congenital pulmonic valve stenosis, which is a partial obstruction of normal blood flow to the lungs, usually due to a malformed pulmonary valve; and canine dilated cardiomyopathy, in which a flaccid heart muscle prevents the organ from pumping properly, ultimately causing congestive heart failure.

Cardiomyopathy is prevalent among Boxers and warrants testing before breeding. Testing is typically performed with a Holter monitor, essentially the same electrocardiogram (ECG) performed on humans. The Holter monitor has attached electrodes that continuously record heart rhythms for 24 consecutive hours. If abnormally frequent or severe ventricular premature contractions (VPCs)—skipped beats or extra beats that don't have a corresponding pulse—are recorded, the dog may have cardiomyopathy. Evidence of VPCs does not always indicate cardiomyopathy; a severe infection can be the culprit. The only way to definitively diagnose cardiomyopathy is to examine the heart tissue under a microscope. This unfortunate disease is incurable; Boxer breeders are highly motivated to have the gene isolated and preclude its inheritance.

Pericardial Disease

The pericardium is a protective sac surrounding the heart and major vessels. Pericardial diseases can be congenital or acquired, requiring different treatments. Pericardial effusion, the most common acquired pericardial disease seen in dogs, is a collection of fluid in the pericardium that impedes cardiac function. Symptoms may include vomiting and labored breathing, or clinical signs may be absent. A stethoscope will detect muffled or displaced heart sounds that will alert the vet to heart trouble, and she may recommend cardiac testing to determine the cause. Effusion is

If your dog does not seem to be feeling well or isn't acting like himself, take him to his vet.

typically treated by inserting a catheter to remove the fluid under the guidance of an echocardiograph (ECG) monitor.

Patent Ductus Arteriosus

Patent ductus arteriosus (PDA) is a birth defect that is the second most common congenital heart defect in dogs. The ductus arteriosus is an open vessel present in the heart of an unborn puppy. It connects the aorta with the pulmonary artery, and it should close after a puppy is born. If it remains open, or *patent*, too much blood is passed into the lungs. Approximately 60 percent of afflicted dogs die within a year of diagnosis. Symptoms include coughing, lethargy, breathing difficulty, and exercise intolerance. If caught early, surgical closure of the duct should result in a normal life for the dog.

Aural Hematomas

An aural hematoma is a swelling of the ear flap, a fairly common problem seen in all breeds, although most often affecting Retrievers. Blood vessels in the ear rupture, causing the space between the skin and the cartilage to fill with blood or serum. The cause is unclear, although underlying issues (ear mites, porcupine quills, allergies) often account for the excess pressure and inflammation. Left untreated, the ear becomes painful, and scarring will occur. Medical treatments don't always succeed but should be attempted before resorting to surgical correction. Your vet can prescribe pain medications to make your Boxer more comfortable.

GENERAL HEALTH ISSUES

Even the healthiest of Boxers will experience some type of health issue during his lifetime. As always, education is the best defense.

Allergies

Allergies typically manifest in three ways: contact, food, and inhalant. With contact allergies, reactions occur when your dog physically touches a substance containing an allergen. Contact allergens include plastic, grass, and wool. Allergy shots are often used to cope with the uncomfortable symptoms, and lifestyle changes may be necessary. A Boxer allergic to his plastic food dish, for example, is easily switched to a steel or ceramic bowl, but the Boxer allergic to grass is more of a challenge. An alternate surface for exercise and relaxation must be provided, such as an enclosed tennis court to run in and a raised dog bed for the backyard. Skin conditions aren't more of a problem for Boxers than for any other breeds, but the dog's coloration can make a difference. White Boxers have more sensitive skin than their fawn and brindle counterparts.

Severe cases of food allergies can produce vomiting and diarrhea. Food allergens must be isolated by trial and error, but once the culprit is found, it's not hard to customize the dog's diet.

Shots and medications, such as antihistamines and steroids, are good for occasional allergy flare-ups, but for ongoing allergy problems, dog owners should investigate other means, like immunotherapy, a treatment designed to desensitize the dog to the allergen by building immunity to it through injections containing small amounts of allergen extract or the allergen itself. Many dogs respond well to this treatment alone, although some may

White Boxers have more sensitive skin than their fawn and brindle counterparts.

need medication in addition to the shots.

Allergies cannot be genetically controlled or predicted, but they can be managed. All it takes is patience and tenacity to identify the problem and the determination to work around it.

Cancer

Canine or human, the very word "cancer" (Latin for "crab") strikes an ominous chord, and with good reason. The incidence of cancer in both species is higher today than ever before. Advances in medicine have afforded both dogs and humans increasing chances for long-term remission, yet cancer remains a relentless nemesis.

Cancer is defined as a proliferation of cell growth and division that results in tumors. It can migrate through the body either systematically through the lymph system or by metastasizing to other sites and forming new tumors, ultimately resulting in death. Boxers have been unfairly considered a high-incidence breed for cancer because of their propensity for tumor development. However, not all tumors are malignant and therefore cancerous; benign tumors are common and usually not life threatening. Cancer can be caused by genetic or environmental factors, or by a random mutation of cells. A dog's individual genetic heritage is a more plausible harbinger of cancer than is his breed. The most we can do to preempt it in our dogs is no different from the precautions we take for ourselves: Eat right, exercise, get regular medical examinations, and watch for possible warning signs, which include:

- anorexia
- bleeding or discharge from any body cavity
- change in elimination
- chronic halitosis
- difficulty breathing
- difficulty eating and/or swallowing
- fatigue and general lethargy
- persistent stiffness or lameness
- sores that won't heal
- unexplained weight loss
- unusual lumps or bumps that grow

A cancer diagnosis is not always a death sentence. Medical treatments have progressed considerably over the last few decades, improving the survival rate of dogs afflicted with this disease. Radiation and chemotherapy are common treatment protocols but can be expensive. You may wish to consider pet health insurance when adding a new dog to your family, keeping in mind that such policies often exclude pre-existing conditions and restrict you to a network of participating veterinarians in which your preferred vet may not be included.

Cancer has become so prevalent in dogs that very few have the good fortune to die in their sleep from old age. Pain management for dogs is trickier than for humans; they are far more stoic about pain than we are and only express it when it becomes severe. It's difficult to gauge a cancer-ridden dog's pain level when he can't answer the familiar question "On a scale of one to ten, your pain is….?" Dog owners today frequently confront the moment of reckoning when their beloved pets' quality

of life no longer justifies keeping them alive. Euthanasia is never an easy decision, even when it's obviously an act of kindness. If your Boxer develops a malignancy, it behooves you to discuss euthanasia with your family and your veterinarian before you have to make that agonizing decision. A clear understanding of the procedure and aftermath is best achieved when you are not overwhelmed by emotion.

Because cancer can be a genetic disease, breeders should not breed dogs whose parents, grandparents, and siblings (even from different litters) develop cancer. This can be difficult, as cancer often doesn't manifest until a dog's senior years, by which time he may have bred already. If your Boxer develops cancer during his lifetime, know that it is not anyone's fault. This disease can strike any dog of any breed at any age. All we can do is provide them with the best care possible and hope for the best.

Ear Disorders

The inside skin of a healthy Boxer's outer ear should be clean, pink, and smooth. If there's an ear problem, your dog will attract your attention with frequent head shaking, scratching, or pawing at his ear. If you detect any irritation, redness, discharge, and/or odor, consult your vet.

An old school of thought once believed that cropped ears were less likely to become infected than uncropped ears because the freer exposure to ambient air discouraged bacterial growth. Not true. Although some breeds with very pendulous ears, like the Basset Hound, may be prone to ear infections because of the continually warm, moist environment inside the ear, the Boxer's natural ear is already fairly short and allows plenty of air circulation.

Ear Mites

The most common ear disorder is ear mite infestation. These tiny parasites usually affect the outer ear canal, although other parts can be affected too. They cause itching and irritation, exacerbated by the dog's inevitable scratching. Ear mites will leave dark brown droppings in the outer ear, coupled with a foul smell. Your vet will prescribe a month-long treatment to flush out the ears and kill any eggs.

Yeast Infections

Yeast inflammation is often a side effect of antibiotics, and it can affect the ears and/or toes. The single-celled organisms rarely cause primary ear infections, but they have no compunction about invading ears already moist and red with irritation, and

A first-aid kit is handy to have in case your Boxer has an emergency.

thus providing a prime breeding ground. Yeast infection is easily identified by a thick, moist, tan to dark brown discharge and a yeasty smell. It causes intense itching, and scratching only worsens the irritation. A common home remedy for yeast infection is a diluted vinegar wash, but vinegar can sting and it won't eradicate the primary cause of the infection. A visit to the vet will solve both issues.

Fly Strike

As the name implies, this condition occurs when biting flies target your Boxer's ears. They may be attracted to the ear by the smell of an infection, ear wax, or a cut or wound. The dog will scratch at the fly bites, worsening the irritation and causing bleeding and/or serous discharge that attracts more flies, thus setting in motion a miserable cycle.

Remove your dog from the area and clean his ears with a vet-recommended product that you may already have on hand. Outside, eliminate flies by removing garbage or any other attraction.

Eye Disorders

Breeders, vets, and breed clubs all share a common quest: to reduce inherited eye disorders. When buying a Boxer from a reputable breeder, you will receive important paperwork that should include medical certificates. One of these should be from the Canine Eye Registration Foundation (CERF), indicating that the Boxer or his parents have been screened for inherited eye diseases like progressive retinal atrophy (PRA).

Progressive Retinal Atrophy

This inherited disorder refers to the degeneration of vision cells in the retina, causing blindness. Early symptoms include loss of night vision, which will make the dog reluctant to go outside at night or into darkened areas outside. Loss of day vision follows, and sometimes cataracts occur. There is no treatment for PRA, which is why annual exams by a veterinary ophthalmologist (the average vet won't have the proper equipment) for PRA are important for breeding stock.

ALTERNATIVE HEALTH CARE THERAPIES

Over the last few decades, many pet owners have become interested in alternative approaches to traditional veterinary care. Alternative or holistic medicine holds that wellness and illness result from combined emotional and physical factors. Ancient disciplines like acupuncture, Reiki, and herbal therapy are frequently utilized in holistic health care, as well as more mainstream treatments like chiropractic and massage therapy.

Holistic medicine advocates the use of natural remedies, usually ingredients found in plants. Holistic veterinarians are slowly becoming more prevalent as greater numbers of traditional veterinarians branch out into alternative treatments. Responsible dog owners should seek an appropriate balance between alternative remedies and scientific medicine, taking advantage of all available resources to ensure a long, healthy life for their Boxers.

Acupuncture

Literally translated as "needle piercing," acupuncture involves inserting very fine needles into the skin to stimulate specific anatomic points in the body for healing purposes. Practiced for centuries by the Chinese, acupuncture is regarded by Western cultures as a complement to traditional medicine. The painless procedure is practiced on dogs by holistic veterinarians for a variety of health issues.

Training Tidbit

If your Boxer wriggles too much for you to effectively perform a tick check, hold a treat in your closed hand and let him sniff it. Keep it in front of his face, encouraging him to stand to expose his whole body. The treat should keep him distracted while you look over his body. When you're finished, reward him with the treat.

Chiropractic

Chiropractic (Greek for "hand practice") is a treatment based on the relationship of the spinal column to the nervous system, biomechanics and movement, and the circulatory system. Chiropractors manipulate the vertebrae to relieve many problems with joints, nerves, and muscles and to alter disease progression. The same principles that bring relief to human patients can help dogs as well.

Herbal Therapy

Humans have used herbs for their curative properties since time immemorial, and the restorative effects are safe for dogs too. Be sure to consult your vet before embarking on any alternative treatment, herbal or

Keep your Boxer's ears clean to prevent infection.

otherwise. Drug interactions, allergic reactions, and herbal product quality are important considerations that you should explore together.

Homeopathy

Based on the principle that "like cures like," homeopathic remedies are made of diluted amounts of the same substance that cause the symptoms in the first place. The theory is that the original substance in highly diluted form stimulates the patient's life force to begin healing. For example, ipecac syrup is used to induce vomiting. In a homeopathic remedy for vomiting, ipecac in very small amounts can relieve vomiting. Veterinary homeopathy can be practiced in conjunction with conventional medical treatment.

Physical Therapy

Modern veterinary practice has mirrored human medical science in improving the quality of life for diseased or maimed dogs. Rehabilitative models commonly used for humans are successfully managing pain and

Many of the same techniques used in human physical therapy are successfully applied to dogs.

restoring mobility for animals whose kindest option was once limited to euthanasia.

Tellington Touch (TTouch)

Perhaps one reason that humans and dogs bond so well is that both species enjoy appropriate touching that evokes trust, rapport, and relaxation. The TTouch is a simple, therapeutic massage technique developed in 1976 by horse trainer and competitive rider Linda Tellington-Jones. Her proven method of applying circular touches with the fingers and hands all over an animal's body has been found to enhance traditional training methods and complement medical treatments.

TTouch motion is performed as though a circle is inscribed on the dog's body. Fingertips are placed on the body and trace a circle from the six o'clock position, past the starting point and completing at the eight o'clock position. Pressure, speed, and circle size are adapted to the particular animal. The "circles" can be applied all over the body, including the gums (performed using two fingers). In addition to circles, TTouch utilizes sliding and rubbing motions that all serve to stimulate the dog's senses and impart relief and/or repose.

Physical Rehabilitation Therapy

Rehabilitation therapy prevents further atrophy of and restores function to an affected body part after injury or surgery. Many of the same techniques used in human physical therapy, such as ultrasound and hydrotherapy, are successfully applied to dogs. Its origins, in relation to dogs, lie in the controversial Greyhound racing industry. Racing Greyhound owners and trainers have been typically reluctant to invest time and money in repairing injuries and rehabilitating dogs unless the latter's pre-injury performance level was fully restored (otherwise healthy Greyhounds no longer considered profitable winners are routinely euthanized or relinquished to shelters, often with untreated wounds and injuries). Physical therapy has become an option for dog owners willing and able to restore a good quality of life to their sick or injured pets.

EMERGENCY CARE

All we humans have to do is dial 911 and an ambulance speeds to our aid. But what happens if your Boxer needs immediate medical attention due to accident or injury? Veterinary ambulances have yet to evolve. Veterinarian house calls are rare, and in a true emergency, impractical. It's best to know how to evaluate an emergency yourself and safely transport your Boxer to the hospital.

First Aid

As the name implies, first aid is the initial treatment you provide your dog immediately following an injury or accident, before you can transport him to the veterinarian. First aid is often life saving, as in cases of profuse bleeding or choking. Purchase a canine emergency first-aid manual and read through it a few times. Don't wait until the accident or emergency happens to read up on what to do. Keep the phone number and driving directions to the nearest after-hours clinic handy.

Bites

Animal bites are a common injury to dogs, unfortunately. If your Boxer receives bites from another dog, contact the owner immediately. Chances are that a neighborhood pet dog has duly received his shots. If the offending dog is a stray without identification, however, you

Dogs are required by law to be vaccinated against rabies, but wild animals are not. Curious Boxers will readily chase a raccoon, fox, or other wild animal whose first defense is biting. These small animals are common rabies carriers, so it is imperative that your Boxer maintain his rabies vaccination schedule.

Snake Bites

Snakes can be dangerous to the curious Boxer, especially venomous species like the copperhead, rattlesnake, and water moccasin. Not surprisingly, most snake bites in dogs are to the head and neck area. If your dog is bitten by a snake, he needs immediate veterinary attention; first-aid attempts in this case are counterproductive. When possible, identify the snake or at least the varieties prevalent in that environment, for the vet's information.

Dogs are required by law to be vaccinated against rabies.

have no way of knowing his veterinary history. If the wounds are superficial, gently cleanse them with warm water and antibacterial soap. Apply an antibiotic ointment to guard against infection. Deep bite wounds may require sutures; take the dog to the vet immediately.

Insect Bites

Dogs who live near farms with livestock are most frequently afflicted by chronic fly bites, sometimes hundreds a day. The flies typically target the thin skin of the ears and bridge of the nose. In addition to causing the dog discomfort, the flies may lay their eggs (body fluids are rich in nutrition for maggots, which is why flies gravitate to decomposing corpses) in the resulting open sores. If your Boxer is the victim of fly strike, remove him from the offending environment and gently cleanse the afflicted area with warm water and a mild antiseptic soap. A topical antibiotic ointment will help prevent infection and relieve pain (if the ointment contains anesthetic properties).

Bites from venomous spiders and stings from bees and scorpions can pose a more serious threat, especially if your dog has an allergic reaction to the sting (called *anaphylaxis*), which can cause respiratory failure. If you suspect that your dog has been bitten or stung, he may need immediate medical attention. Try to locate the culprit and collect it in a sealed jar or plastic bag. You'll take it with you to the vet, who can then determine the appropriate antivenin, if necessary. Apply a pressure bandage to the bite site to retard the venom's systemic distribution. If a leg has been bitten, try to apply a splint to immobilize it, as movement accelerates the venom's spread. If you can safely lift your Boxer, carry him to the car while you speak calmly to him. A large Boxer may require you to solicit someone's help and use a large blanket as a sling to carry him to the vehicle.

Bleeding
Profuse external bleeding takes precedence over other injuries and must be addressed at once. Depending on severity, a pressure bandage applied to the wound or a tourniquet (reserved only for the unstoppable bleeding) tied between the wound and the heart can prevent shock from blood loss. Transport the dog to a veterinarian immediately.

Internal bleeding indicates a severe problem but is obviously more difficult to detect. A dog bleeding internally may have very pale gums; produce bloody sputum; bleed from the nose, mouth, or rectum; produce bloody stool or urine; or collapse. If you notice any of these signs in your Boxer, keep him warm and quiet while you seek immediate veterinary advice.

Broken Bones
Warning signs of fracture include limping, using only three legs, swelling, localized pain, difficult breathing, or frothy breath. If your Boxer has fallen or experienced an accident in which you suspect he has broken a bone, immobilize the limb with a makeshift splint to prevent further damage. Newspaper sections work well when wrapped around the limb and taped together. For the size of an adult Boxer, a slim piece of wood tied against the limb with strips of cloth will suffice to immobilize a broken leg. If ribs are broken and protrude through the skin, cover the area with a wet cloth to keep out dirt and debris, and watch for bleeding. Transport him to the vet immediately.

Frostbite
Frostbite occurs when skin tissues are exposed to extremely cold temperatures and ice crystals form within the cells, rupturing and ultimately killing them. Sometimes accompanying hypothermia (excessively low body temperature), frostbite can affect dogs on their extremities—toes, ears, scrotum, and tail tip—just as it affects humans. As the blood supply to the affected area diminishes, the skin will become pale. It will turn red, swell, and become itchy and

Keep your Boxer out of harm's reach—never allow him access to poisonous substances, indoors or out

painful when blood circulation returns during treatment. In severe cases that produce necrotic (dead) tissue, amputation may be necessary to prevent potentially fatal gangrene infection.

If you suspect that your Boxer is suffering from frostbite, and you cannot seek immediate veterinary assistance, warm the frozen body part in a tub of warm water at 104° to 108°F (40° to 42.2°C). However, if there is a risk of the thawed extremity refreezing, do not attempt to warm it or you risk more acute tissue damage. It is

better to leave the part frozen until you can get indoors. Do not attempt to thaw a frozen extremity over a fire or heater. Lack of sensation creates a risk of burns, which will dehydrate injured tissue and exacerbate the damage. Nor should you rub the afflicted area, which can further damage fragile tissue.

Heatstroke (Hyperthermia)

Dogs do not sweat like we do, although they perspire a little through their paws. Their primary cooling method is panting, which exchanges hot air for cool air. The risk of heatstroke occurs in situations where there just isn't much cool air. When a Boxer needs to cool off, he'll pant with a tongue that appears larger than usual. It swells to increase its surface area and allow more air to pass over it. The blood vessels in the tongue then distribute the cooled blood through the body.

Prevention is the best way to combat heatstroke. Canine cooling systems are not as efficient as the human body's, leaving dogs more susceptible to hyperthermia. Boxers are especially at risk due to their brachycephalic heads. You should suspect heatstroke if your Boxer is exposed to very hot temperatures, even for a short time, and exhibits the following symptoms:

- dazed expression
- increased heart/pulse rate
- moisture accumulating on feet
- rapid mouth breathing
- reddened gums
- thickened saliva
- vomiting

Heatstroke requires immediate action to save the dog's life. For mild cases, remove him to a cooler environment and give him cool (not cold) water to drink. If he seems unsteady on his feet or has a high temperature, put him in a cool bath or shower. Applying ice packs to his head, chest, and thighs will accelerate a decrease in body temperature. See a vet immediately.

Poisoning

Poisoning occurs when a substance is ingested or absorbed that injures health or causes death. Our world is filled with poisons, chemical and natural. No matter how conscientious we are about safeguarding them from these dangers, our pets are sometimes exposed.

Here is an overview of some of the commonest poisons lurking in our dogs' surroundings.

Indoor Poisons
- common foods like chocolate, onions, grapes, raisins, macadamia nuts, and others
- cosmetics and perfumes
- household cleaners
- poisonous houseplants, such as chrysanthemums and poinsettias
- prescription and nonprescription medications and dietary supplements on countertops and vanities
- toilet bowl continuous sanitizers

Outdoor Poisons
- common outdoor plants, like the rhododendron and lady's slipper orchids
- pesticides, herbicides, and insecticides such as slug bait, Japanese beetle traps, rodent traps and killers, weed killers
- some snakes, some spiders, scorpions, and stinging winged insects

Garage Poisons
- antifreeze
- car cleaning products
- exposed insulation
- gasoline
- paint and paint thinners
- sharp gardening or landscaping implements

CHAPTER 9

BOXER TRAINING

All dogs need training and socialization to help them learn about and adapt their behavior to the world around them. One of the cornerstones of responsible dog ownership is control of your dog at all times, and the best control comes from a close bond of friendship and mutual trust between you and your dog, a bond that is formed and strengthened by good training. When you combine the Boxer's strong physique with his natural intelligence, curiosity, and tenacity, you get a dog who needs training perhaps even more so than other breeds. A well-trained Boxer is a happy, confident dog who is welcome wherever he goes. His training can range from basic obedience commands (like *sit*, *down*, and *stay*, described in Chapter 4), to more advanced work in competitive obedience.

Boxers historically assisted humans as they went to war, hunted, and worked with livestock as butchers and ranchers. As members of the American Kennel Club (AKC) Working Group and the United Kennel Club (UKC) Guardian Group of breeds, with proper training Boxers continue to serve humans professionally in security and law enforcement. Recreationally, the Boxer's industrious, competitive nature perfectly suits him for organized dog activities like conformation and Schützhund.

Boxers are so anxious to please that they are quite easily trained. The bond formed early between you and your Boxer during training will go a long way in developing a relationship in which he knows what you expect of him and is happy to oblige.

HEEL

Because of the Boxer's natural strength, the *heel* is an important command to learn because it will help you have control of your Boxer at all times. Pre-heeling training begins with a young puppy learning to follow his owner while walking off leash. Once he's ready to progress to on-leash walking, you can start teaching the *heel*.

Want to Know More?

If your Boxer needs a refresher on how to walk nicely on leash, see Chapter 4: Training Your Puppy.

How to Teach the *Heel*

1. Attach the leash to your Boxer's collar.
2. Put your Boxer in a *sit* position next to your left foot.
3. Step off with your left foot, saying "Heel." If he doesn't respond, slap the coils of the extra leash against your leg to encourage movement. Keep walking.
4. As long as he remains next to you, praise him. If he stops or veers away, start over.
5. End with a *sit* command, praise, and then a treat.

STAY

Stay is no doubt the most crucial command for your Boxer to learn. Don't skimp on mastering this command; it could prevent him from engaging in a serious altercation or getting into a dangerous situation, like running into traffic. The challenge is teaching it to a breed that wants to be right by your side every minute. You've also taught him to follow you with the *heel* command; how do you now train him to do the opposite?

How to Teach the *Sit-Stay*

The *sit-stay* command informs your Boxer that he will remain in the *sit* position a bit longer than the one-second "please?" duration he's learned to assume before receiving food or going through a doorway. He must now learn that *stay*—regardless of position— means that he must hold the *sit* until you tell him otherwise.

Mealtime is a convenient means of teaching the *sit-stay*, because your Boxer has already learned to sit before he may eat.

1. This time when he sits, keep the food bowl in your other hand out of reach and give the verbal command "Stay," holding your open palm like a "stop" signal in front of his face.
2. Start to put the bowl down; if he moves, interrupt him with a "No" or other vocal

A Boxer who has learned to heel is a pleasure to take on walks.

warning and raise the bowl out of reach again. Be ready to grab the bowl if he darts for it.

3. Start the process again with a *sit* command, stay command, and bowl placement until he successfully waits for the release word okay before moving. He only has to maintain the *sit-stay* one second for the exercise to be successful.

Gradually extend the wait time, but not longer than 30 seconds; the goal isn't to tease the dog unnecessarily. This exercise works well at doorways, too; the dog will learn that not only must he wait until the pack leader (you) goes through the doorway first, but that he can't move from his *sit* position until the pack leader verbally releases him.

Another training exercise for the *sit-stay* utilizes the leash and makes a good companion to the mealtime and doorway exercises:

1. Leash your Boxer with a long training lead for control purposes. Most of the lead will be gathered in your hand during the exercise.

2. Put him in a *sit* position next to your left foot.

3. When he is sitting, firmly say "Stay!" and hold your left palm in front of his face.

4. Step off with your right foot, and bring your left palm in front of his face. If he steps out with you, stop him and start over with the sit position until he understands that he should remain in the sit, regardless of your movements.

5. When he holds the position, release him with "Okay!" and a treat.

6. End with a *sit* command, praise, and then treat.

As he masters the concept, extend the distance you create between you two: a few steps away, walking around him in a close circle, the full length of the leash, dropping the leash, and ultimately off-leash. Remember that control of your dog at all times is imperative, so train the off-leash phase in a secured area.

Down-Stay

The *down-stay* is an important progression in your Boxer's training because it solidifies his relationship with you. A dog in the *down-stay* isn't being submissive, as he would be by rolling on his back and baring his vulnerable underbelly. By maintaining a passive *down* position, he is demonstrating his trust of your authority. Teaching this command is much like teaching the *sit-stay*.

The *down–stay* solidifies your Boxer's relationship with you.

How to Teach the *Down-Stay* Command:

1. Begin with your Boxer in a *down*, next to your left leg. Keep his head slightly raised with gentle pressure on the leash.
2. While he is down, firmly say "Stay!" and step forward with your right foot.
3. At the same time, bring your left palm in front of his face. If he attempts to go with you, stop him and start over with the *down* position.
4. Repeat "Stay" or "Good stay" as you distance yourself, while keeping an eye on him.
5. After he demonstrates in a few subsequent practice sessions that he understands what you want him to do, add small distractions such as approaching him after distancing yourself and walking around him and away again. Progress to a level of obedience where he maintains the *down-stay* without a leash in a restricted area, remembering that control at all times is essential. Praise him and pet him when you're close. Don't prolong the practice sessions, and always end with a *sit*, praise, and a treat.

STAND

Mastering the *stand* command comes in handy at veterinary exams and grooming sessions and is a requisite for conformation competition. It is taught in basically the same way as the *sit-stay* and *down-stay*.

How to Teach the *Stand*

1. Begin with your Boxer in the *sit* position.
2. Present a treat just out of his reach, and draw it farther away, saying "Stand."
3. Keep your hand placed under your Boxer's belly to keep him still and reward him with his treat and praise.

As always, begin and end this not-too-long practice session with *sit*, praise, and a treat.

FORMAL TRAINING CLASSES

The Boxer is a strong dog with a high intelligence level. In inexperienced hands, he may not get the training he needs to become a happy and safe member of the family. Your Boxer may have a great "stay" in your backyard, but are you sure he'll react the same way at a dog park or around strangers? Unless you are an experienced dog trainer who has worked with Boxers before, you may find enrolling in a formal training program— whether for private instruction or group classes—the best way to train your Boxer.

No matter which training environment you choose, be sure there's a good fit between you, your dog, and the instructor. Observe different classes to see if you and your Boxer will be comfortable with that instructor's methods. Look for the following:

- Are the dogs in the class enjoying themselves?
- Does the instructor handle the dogs in a way you would want your Boxer handled?
- Are the dogs and humans paying attention to the instructor?

Group Classes

Consider the pros and cons of group classes versus private obedience instruction. In a group, the dog must learn how to behave around distractions, namely the other dogs and people in the class. Considering that you want your Boxer to remain in your control at all times, no matter what distractions occur, this might be a good choice for you. Your dog may even find some future playmates among his classmates. The downside of group classes is that the distractions sometimes prove too much for certain dogs.

Private Lessons

For dogs who have trouble concentrating, individual lessons might be in order. Sometimes, a few private lessons are all that the dog needs to join a group class later. For obvious reasons, one-on-one lessons are better for dogs with aggression or other behavioral problems. Private lessons may also be the only type of training busy dog owners can fit into their schedules.

CHAPTER 10

BOXER PROBLEM BEHAVIORS

Sometimes the very qualities we admire in a Boxer are channeled in negative ways. Loyalty may manifest in aggression; love for humans may manifest in separation anxiety; intelligence may lead to boredom and subsequent destructive behaviors like digging and chewing. If a Boxer's bad behavior deteriorates to a level where safety is in question, you must take immediate action to rectify the problem and prevent legal intervention. All it takes is one person's complaint to a local animal control division to establish a record flagging your dog as potentially dangerous, even though it's untrue. If further complaints are registered, you may be required to muzzle your Boxer whenever he leaves your property.

Even the best-behaved dogs have their moments. No matter how well trained your Boxer is, there will come a time where he doesn't do the right thing. And it's always possible that your adopted or rescued Boxer with a shady past may exhibit behaviors incongruent with the appropriate training and care he now receives from you. Learning to recognize potentially habitual, unwanted behaviors is your first step toward correcting them for good.

AGGRESSION

Aggression is unwarranted, antagonistic behavior directed at people or other animals. It can manifest in varying degrees, with the mildest being a throaty growl of warning and the worst, a physical attack. Aggression is the most serious problem behavior because of its obvious danger to others and the legal repercussions it can provoke, including euthanasia. It must be confronted at the first sign, for an aggressive dog will easily detect his humans' uncertainty or fear and use it to cement his superiority over them.

Aggression can take many forms or manifest under certain circumstances that seem illogical to us. For instance, a dog in a one-pet home with no competition for food may display aggression toward anyone who approaches his eating area. Seeking professional help is the wisest course, as behaviorists recognize the many faces of aggression, how to treat them, and even assess if a dog's aggression is so severe that rehabilitation isn't possible.

Territorial Aggression

This type of hostility is directed at any person or animal that enters into what the dog considers his space, whether it's the yard, home, or his

Seeking Professional Help

For serious behavioral issues, like aggression, you may wish to seek professional help. Just as humans look to psychiatrists and psychologists for help with their own emotional and mental issues, problem dogs work with animal behaviorists, professionals who assess and treat companion animals to rectify, when possible, a negative behavior. If your Boxer exhibits a negative behavior that you believe warrants professional intervention, you need to know the specifics of animal behavior professionals and what they do.

Veterinary behaviorists are veterinarians who have received extensive training in the field of animal behavior, above and beyond veterinary school. They are board certified by the American College of Veterinary Behaviorists (ACVB), an institution dedicated to promoting the welfare of animals and the human–animal bond through the use of positive, proven methods of behavior modification. This certification is similar to the specific, standardized education and training that human physicians receive in their chosen fields of specialty and distinguishes veterinary behaviorists from more generalized animal behaviorists.

Animal behaviorists come from a variety of educational and experiential milieux, with a broad background in general animal behavior theory and application. Their focus isn't necessarily on dogs alone or even on companion animals. They are not necessarily veterinarians, although many veterinarians with an interest in veterinary behavior become certified animal behaviorists. Sanction by the Animal Behavior Society Program for Certification of Applied Animal Behaviorists (CAAB) attests to the participants' professionalism and dedication to animal welfare. Animal behaviorists are the "general practitioners," while veterinary behaviorists are the "psychiatrists."

The simplest way to find a behavior specialist is by asking your regular veterinarian for a referral. You may also seek referrals from the ACBV or the American

Veterinary Medical Association (AVMA), the veterinary equivalent of the American Medical Association (AMA). Organizations like these have comprehensive websites that usually include directories of their members and/or diplomates. If no veterinary behaviorist is in reasonable proximity, you may consult the Animal Behavior Society (ABS) for their list of animal-behaviorist members. If a neighbor or other layperson refers you to a local animal behaviorist, research the latter's credentials for proper education and training. The last place you want to turn for help with a dog's problem behavior is to a self-styled "expert," or worse, a scam artist.

Before you make an initial appointment with a behaviorist, call or stop by for information on her treatment philosophies and protocols. Compile a checklist of questions, such as:

- How long is the typical appointment? Sixty to 90 minutes is usual.

- Whose attendance is required? All family members involved should attend.

- What will take place during the first appointment? A qualified professional behaviorist should garner detailed information of your Boxer's health history, history of the current problem, and any steps you may have taken already.

- How many appointments will be necessary to complete treatment? Six weekly meetings are typical.

- What special equipment, if any, is used during treatment? Find out exactly what items, such as a pronged collar or ultrasonic device, may be utilized. Do not agree to any procedure with which you are uncomfortable.

- What type of severe physical treatment will my dog undergo during therapy? The only acceptable answer is "none." A qualified behavior professional should never hit, shake, knee, kick, jerk, or otherwise use harsh corporal treatment for behavior modification.

- What is the cost of the entire treatment protocol? It couldn't hurt to compare costs with other qualified, reputable behaviorists in your area.

- What if the problem behavior recurs after completion of treatment? Ask if treatment fees include follow-up appointments and/or additional treatment within a certain time frame.

Even the best-behaved dogs have their moments of trouble.

human's car. The intense barking and/or teeth baring that warns "intruders" against crossing boundaries is passively reinforced when the person or animal moves on, such as a neighbor walking past a fence. Territorial behavior may escalate to snapping and biting if the perimeter is breached. Owners of territorial Boxers should seek professional help immediately.

Rehabilitation options include neutering (if the aggressive dog is an intact male), supervision, and mastering the *down-stay* command when visitors come to the door. With patience and consistency, most territorial aggression can be unlearned.

Dog Aggression

Boxers who adore their humans but do not tolerate other dogs are called dog aggressive,

a trait not unusual in the "bully" breeds—a generalized term for breeds like the Boxer, Bulldog, Bull Terrier, American Bulldog, American Staffordshire Terrier—with a common ancestry in fighting and bullbaiting. Dog aggression is often blamed on a lack of early socialization or when a puppy less than eight weeks old is taken from his mother and littermates, before he's had a chance to experience appropriate pack hierarchy and behavior with them. Sometimes, though, dog aggression can erupt in spite of appropriate environmental factors. For instance, two Boxers of the same sex in the same household can battle for dominance without resolution if neither capitulates. They can develop a lifelong grudge against each other and require permanent separation. If they are males, neutering can help diffuse the tension; however, spaying females does not produce the same effect.

Most dog-aggressive Boxers can benefit from professional intervention and treatment. In most cases, a dog can be taught to calmly ignore other dogs he encounters, even those who might challenge him, with extensive obedience training that focuses on the *down-stay*, a position of passivity.

Human Aggression

Boxers are not aggressive toward humans without good reason, and an aggressive temperament can disqualify a puppy from a career in conformation. Adult Boxers —especially those rescued or adopted—may display aggression toward all humans or specific classes of people, such as people in uniform, children, or men. This is not uncommon in cases of prior abuse. If your Boxer displays any signs of human aggression, seek professional help immediately.

Subtypes of human aggression include :

- **fear aggression:** occurs when a dog reacts to a fearful situation or trigger
- **possessive aggression:** occurs when a dog aggressively reacts to someone reaching for his toy or food
- **dominance aggression:** occurs when a dog refuses to accede to his human's leadership position and poses a continual safety threat
- **predatory aggression:** occurs when a dog views humans as prey; this is the most unpredictable and dangerous form of

Although some Boxers can be dog aggressive, many are not and enjoy the company of other dogs.

A Boxer left along for long stretches may bark to get some attention or because he is bored.

aggression, the origins of which are not clearly understood; this is rare in Boxers

- **pain aggression:** occurs when an injured or sick dog, unsure of an approaching human's intentions, naturally snaps at or bites him; this is not a temperament flaw but an instinct forged long ago in the wild, where sick or injured dogs became easy prey themselves.

BARKING

A Boxer's bark vocalizes his moods. A happy-sounding bark while in the play bow means that he's having fun. A high-pitched yelp might indicate pain or fear. A low, throaty bark, often heard during certain kinds of play, may be a warning to back off.

Barking isn't a punishable offense. It can be a good thing, especially if unwelcome strangers are around. Boxers aren't known to be excessive barkers, but there are always exceptions. A Boxer's watchdog instincts may be in overdrive, or he may be bored and lonely. If barking becomes excessive and habitual, behavior modification is in order.

A Boxer left alone every day for long stretches may discover that barking brings attention. Even the negative attention of a neighbor yelling at him to shut up is better than no attention. When you're at home together, take steps to encourage your Boxer to be quiet.

Management Technique

1. If he starts barking for no reason, tell him in a sharp voice, "Quiet!" Mentally count to three, letting the command and effect sink

in, and if he hasn't resumed barking, reward him with a treat.

2. When he has mastered this command, leave the house for a short walk outside by yourself to see how he responds. Make these departures and arrivals low profile to discourage barking from excitement—no dramatic farewells or greetings. If he barks, calm him down with another "Quiet!" and a treat if he passes the three-count test.

3. Take the modification a step further by leaving the house and talking with a neighbor outside where your Boxer can see you. If he barks in protest of this social exclusion, correct him as before. Repeat these steps as necessary until he learns when not to bark.

A radical solution to problem barking is surgical debarking. Performed under general anesthesia, this procedure reduces the tissue in the dog's vocal chords, affecting the volume and tone of the bark but not the desire and ability to vocalize. Debarking is most often performed on herding breeds like Collies and Shelties, whose naturally loud, ear-piercing bark is important to their work. Herding dogs historically barked to scare off predators from flocks or fish drying in the sun. Times may have changed, but the barking instinct in certain breeds has not.

Fortunately, Boxers are usually not problem barkers. A Boxer owner considering surgical debarking should realize that the procedure can actually backfire. If scar tissue forms, it can produce a harsh noise similar to a smoker's cough and even more annoying than before. Such a radical step should be taken only as a last-resort solution for a dog facing homelessness or euthanasia due to excessive barking.

CHEWING

Chewing is mostly a problem with teething puppies. They can and will chew anything they can get their teeth on, so it behooves you to make inaccessible anything that you value or that can hurt your puppy, such as electric cords. Adult dogs also enjoy chewing, and the correct chew toys help maintain healthy teeth and gums.

Management Technique

The best way to prevent unwanted chewing is to provide lots of safe chew toys, like Nylabones, to keep your Boxer occupied. A safe chew toy is one that doesn't splinter, break, or tear, possibly causing internal injuries if consumed. A wide variety of palatable chew toys are available with different flavors, textures, and sizes to appeal to even the most discriminating Boxer.

An adult Boxer who chews inappropriately may be experiencing separation anxiety or may simply be bored without the company of his humans. He may benefit from the mental stimulation of a chew toy that dispenses treats from certain openings or that plays a comforting message, pre-recorded in your voice, when motion activated. If intriguing chew toys don't work, you may need to confine your dog to a chew-proofed area. The reliable crate is the safest way to protect both your Boxer and your belongings.

Want to Know More?

For a refresher on intermediate commands that can help resolve problem behaviors, see Chapter 9: Boxer Training.

DIGGING

Although humans view digging as destructive, this behavior comes very naturally to dogs. Domesticated dogs are free of the burden of finding food and shelter, but not of the instinct to do so. Moreover, dirt and soil are endless sources of tempting smells that Boxers can't resist pursuing. Some dogs even dig out of boredom.

Management Technique

To correct inappropriate digging, you must catch your dog in the act, which can be tricky, especially since you're usually either away or busy inside when the digging is in progress. By the time you notice the holes or decimated flower beds, it's too late to chastise. Your Boxer won't connect a reprimand with something he did hours earlier. If you are willing to keep a vigil while your Boxer is in the yard, you can verbally interrupt him if he starts to dig. This requires a time commitment that most people are unable to maintain for the duration of training.

It may be easier to embrace your digger than to change his behavior. Create a digging space especially for your Boxer by fencing off a section of the yard where you can leave him to dig to his heart's content.

A well-socialized dog will have fewer problem behaviors than a dog who has not been socialized.

Food Stealing

You may think that a food item placed far back on the kitchen counter is out of your Boxer's reach, but this breed is determined and enterprising. They can be notorious food thieves.

Management Technique

To discourage this behavior, make the reward less rewarding. Make a shaker can using an empty soda can and a handful of coins or pebbles. Place it on the counter right near the food temptation, positioned to fall when your dog pulls down the food. He will associate the startling noise with the action and reconsider a life of crime.

Alternatively, you can purchase motion-activated devices that work on the same principle. Place the device on the counter with the food; it will emit a loud noise when the dog (or anyone else, for that matter) comes too close or touches the device.

JUMPING ON PEOPLE

Boxers love people, love jumping, and love to do both at once. A puppy attempting to jump up in greeting is adorable, but a 50-pound (22.5-kg) adult Boxer jumping up on someone can be frightening and precarious. At the very least, it's inconsiderate; hosiery and delicate fabrics are not Boxer-resistant.

Management Technique

Jumping on people can be prevented with early training of the *sit* command.

1. When you enter the house, resist the urge to greet your Boxer until you have a leash and collar in hand. Slip the collar on and tell him to sit.
2. If he jumps up in excitement, say "No" firmly and put him back in a *sit*. Avoid saying the word "down" so that you don't confuse him with the command to lie down.
3. When he sits nicely and is quiet, reward him with a treat to reinforce the message that attention and other good things come his way only if he sits.

Another way to correct unwanted jumping is to stop it before it starts. If your Boxer is excited, and you think that he is about to jump on you, just walk away. If he jumps before you get the chance to leave, raise your knee as a passive barrier only. His chest will bump against it but he won't be hurt. Be mindful not to use the knee to forcibly push him away or hit him. The idea is to thwart his action, not inflict pain. Pay no attention to him until he's

Training Tidbit

sitting quietly, then lavish him with praise and affection. Once he learns that jumping on people doesn't achieve the desired response, he will lose the motivation to continue the behavior.

Get in the habit of putting your Boxer into a *sit* before he does anything pleasurable, like eating a meal, going for a walk, or fetching a ball. He will see that if he sits for an approaching visitor, praise and attention will follow. Enlist the help of visitors by asking them to refrain from petting your dog until he sits so that he isn't "rewarded" for incorrect behavior. In public, explain to anyone who asks to pet him to wait until the dog sits, as you're trying to teach him good manners. Even one instance of petting after jumping on someone can hamper progress if the dog decides that the possibility of attention is worth the risk of incorrect behavior.

LEASH PULLING

Leash pulling during walks is detrimental for several reasons:

- Your leadership position is undermined if the dog is allowed to lead you.
- You appear to be without control of your dog, which can make others uneasy.
- A strong adult Boxer can easily pull off balance a child, petite adult, or fragile senior citizen.

Management Technique

If you walk a dog who pulls on his leash, he is literally walking you. He thinks that he is the leader who sets the pace and direction. He will enjoy the walk much more without that responsibility.

Clicker training is an effective, positive way to remedy leash-pulling behavior (or use your marker word). Treat rewards for desired

behavior are accompanied by a simultaneous click. Eventually, the treat is removed from the equation and the clicking sound is accompanied by lavish praise when a desired behavior is performed. The dog learns that certain actions evoke the clicking sound, associated at first with treats and ultimately with praise.

1. Start with your leashed dog in a *sit* position at your left side.
2. Give him a confident command like "Let's go" or "Let's take a walk" as you step out.
3. As he steps out apace with you, give praise, a click, and a treat. If he starts to pull ahead, get his attention with a click and a "Watch me!" or "Pay attention!"

Jumping on people can be prevented with early training of the sit command.

Good leash manners are a must, especially with a large dog like the Boxer.

4. When he stops and looks at you, click and reward. Offer lavish verbal praise as he walks nicely at your side.

5. If he starts to veer in a different direction but isn't pulling, tighten the lead's slack just until he feels the restriction, motivating him to return to your left side. He may need a "Watch me!' reinforcement.

6. Click and reward every time he takes the correct action.

This training can also be performed without the clicker, using just treat lures. Hold an aromatic treat like a small piece of hot dog in your left hand. Hold it out in front of the dog's nose as you say "Let's go." He will track the scent by remaining at your side as you walk, for which you should praise him and offer the reward. As you progress with this exercise, eliminate the treat lure and obtain his compliance for praise and affection.

Mounting

Mounting behavior is not the same as mounting for sexual intercourse. Males and females alike are known to mount, and neutering or spaying does not necessarily eliminate this conduct. It is most often directed toward humans and other dogs, but mounting

A well-behaved Boxer is a pleasure to live with.

can also involve objects like pillows and toy stuffed animals. The behavior is harmless in itself; people may find it a source of embarrassment or amusement.

Contrary to popular belief, mounting behavior usually has nothing to do with sex or dominance. Dogs are exuberant creatures; mounting often occurs in situations of nonsexual stimulation or excitement. The behavior is not uncommon among adolescent dogs, and often ceases naturally upon reaching maturity.

Management Technique

If mounting behavior doesn't resolve itself, try distraction. When you see your dog mounting, say "No!" firmly and gently remove him from the mounting posture. If he persists, distract him with another activity. Be careful not to give him anything that might be misconstrued as a treat or reward; you'll only reinforce the mounting behavior. One idea might be to practice a few basic obedience commands. If all else fails, you can calmly remove him to his crate for a "time-out" that is diverting rather than punitive. Avoid displays of displeasure or anger that might inadvertently link the crate to punishment. If the mounting behavior persists past adolescence, consult your veterinarian. Sometimes hormonal issues may be responsible.

NIPPING

To puppies, nipping is nothing more than a fun game played with their littermates. But it's hardly fun for the humans they nip in the same playful manner. Nose and ear cartilage are nice and chewy, but those needle-sharp puppy teeth hurt! More to the point, puppies who playfully nip their humans are treating them as pack equals. Their mother may tolerate a nip here and there, but if they go too far she will readily chastise her pups as their authority figure. They learn to respect her and the boundaries she establishes.

Dogs must learn the same respect for their humans and realize that their position is

low on the family totem pole. It is easy for a Boxer to view human children in the family as peers, especially when they run and jump around in much the same way that a puppy plays. Nipping is also a means of establishing dominance. The Boxer must learn that biting or nipping humans is unacceptable under any circumstances.

Management Technique

Nipping tends to abate considerably when pups grow out of the teething stage. Meanwhile, there are steps you can take to discourage nipping.

1. Provide your Boxer with plenty of appropriate chew toys.
2. If he nips one of his humans during play, say "No" firmly and immediately substitute an appropriate chew toy for your hand, nose, arm, or whatever part of you he nipped.
3. Remember to discourage improper behavior by encouraging appropriate behavior. Gentle mouthing during play with humans is fine, but it is not instinctive. The goal is to teach him to control the force of his nipping.

Never hit or smack a puppy for nipping. He may misinterpret it as play behavior and the problem will worsen. Or he may learn to fear you, creating other, more serious problem behaviors. Don't hesitate to consult your vet for advice on how to discourage nipping behavior. If you have young children, she may suggest involving them in the training so that they learn to respect boundaries as well.

Multi-Dog Tip

Multi-dog owners see their fair share of behavioral issues, mostly surrounding dominance. You'll often be advised to let antagonistic dogs resolve differences for themselves. This seems logical when you ponder the concept of pack hierarchy, but peaceable resolution isn't guaranteed. If you notice a lingering animosity between two of your dogs or uncharacteristic behavior exhibited by one or more, consult a behaviorist to help you understand the underlying root of the problem.

CHAPTER 11

BOXER SPORTS AND ACTIVITIES

We've already established that the high-energy Boxer requires regular, vigorous exercise to stay healthy and happy. We've also established that the Boxer's intelligence and desire to please his humans make him a very trainable dog. Put it all together, and you have a breed that is well suited to a wide variety of organized activities and sports you may already enjoy or would like to try.

BOXER ACTIVITIES

The Boxer's steadfast love of his humans makes him more than willing to share in your leisure activities, as long as he's physically able. There is no reason why you can't include your healthy Boxer in some of your favorite outdoor pursuits.

Camping

Whether you're pitching a tent or enjoying the creature comforts of an RV, your Boxer is a welcome addition to the party. If you're planning to stay at an organized campsite, such as those under the auspices of Kampgrounds of America (KOA), you should determine beforehand if pets are allowed. An organization like KOA may be pet friendly, but individual campsites may have their own policies regarding pets. Some may have restrictions on certain breeds that are generalized as aggressive. Unfortunately, the Boxer may be included in this group as one of the maligned "bully" breeds that share an ancestry of fighting, baiting, and warring and are therefore still considered—unfairly—to be dangerous or vicious. Although unjust, it's best not to flout these policies and put a troublesome spotlight on your Boxer. At campsites where your Boxer is welcome, make sure that his behavior is circumspect and that you leave the grounds cleaner than you found them. All it takes is one careless camper who doesn't clean up after her dog to compel the campsite to ban pets altogether.

Practice Advance Planning

If you're a hiker who wants to take your Boxer along on the trail, practice the same kind of advance planning. Contact the park service or local administration where you plan to hike to confirm that dogs are allowed on the trails. Follow all rules to the letter to ensure that dogs continue to be welcome in the parks and on the trails.

If you have a white Boxer, apply a sunscreen formulated for babies when enjoying the outdoors together.

Outfit Your Hiking Partner

Once you're clear on permission, focus on outfitting your hiking partner with his own equipment. A backpack especially designed for dogs will carry most of his supplies. Minimalist backpacks resemble the vests worn by service dogs and are obviously lighter and cooler for a Boxer to wear. More demanding hikes (although never more demanding than a dog can reasonably handle) call for more supplies and larger, more intricate dog backpacks to carry them. A wide variety of dog backpacks and vests are on the market now, including breed-specific models. Even though you're sure that your Boxer is healthy and in good physical shape, he must be conditioned gradually to wearing a loaded backpack.

A dog in good shape can typically carry 10 to 15 percent of his body weight in a backpack. The Boxer's muscular build may enable him to carry as much as 25 percent of his weight, but you don't want to undermine his comfort and stamina on an outing that is supposed to be fun.

Take Precautions

Similarly, you will maximize the activity's enjoyment by taking a few simple precautions:

- Apply a topical flea/tick preventive a day or so prior to the outing.
- If your Boxer is white, apply a sunscreen formulated for babies.
- If you use a retractable leash on hikes

to allow your Boxer a little freedom to explore along the trail, take along a nylon lead as backup. The cord of a retractable leash can break under the pull of a strong, excited adult Boxer.

- Remember to pack a collapsible bowl for water breaks.
- Ensure that the outside temperature during your hike is temperate enough for a Boxer.

Walking and Jogging

Walking is more than just a pleasant activity or an elimination opportunity for your Boxer. Dogs are pack animals for whom walking defines their very survival. In the wild, dogs walk all day in search of food; they walk whenever and wherever the alpha dog leads. For a Boxer, walking becomes even more important. Aside from his high energy level that should be expended in daily physical activity, walking is important to his mental balance by fulfilling his working-dog instincts. A Boxer is happiest when he's performing the job he was bred for: protection of his humans.

Pack Leadership

Walking with your Boxer is an activity that involves much more than just hooking on a leash and heading out. It's an expression of your firm position as pack leader in your Boxer's life. A happy dog is one who is secure in the knowledge of his position within his pack: below yours. Therefore, a controlled walk in which your Boxer stays by your side at all times, matches his pace to yours, and ignores everything and everyone encountered until you give him leave is not unfair or punitive. Without free rein to forge ahead of you and assume, albeit temporarily, an alpha position on the walk, your Boxer is liberated from the responsibility of leading

and protecting you. The controlled walk then becomes a Boxer's enjoyable excursion with his human, not a reconnaissance mission.

Boxer owners can benefit from working with a professional trainer on controlled walking on such points as:

- the appropriate-sized collar
- the appropriate type of leash
- how to administer corrections properly when your Boxer makes mistakes on walks, such as running ahead of you, barking and pulling at the sight of another dog, or jumping up on someone you meet
- awareness of your surroundings at all times
- when to allow freedom to explore, and how to regain control
- how to carry yourself to exude confidence and leadership

Training should include ancillary behavior that you, as pack leader, must practice at all times to foster enjoyable, stress-free walks.

Don't Label Your Pet as a Service Dog

No matter what type of gear you buy for your outdoor companion, be sure that it bears none of the identifications or markings of a service dog. It is illegal and unethical to label your pet as a service dog if you are not disabled. On-duty service dogs of various breeds are often identified as "working" to discourage the public from greeting, petting, or otherwise distracting them. A Boxer's American Kennel Club (AKC) classification as a breed in the Working Group does not equate him to a working dog serving his disabled owner.

Walking with your Boxer is a good way to bond with him and establish your role as pack leader.

The leader always precedes the dog through any doorway, even inside your home. The leader doesn't provoke overstimulation by asking her Boxer in a high, excited voice, "Oh, boy, who wants to go for a walk?" Collar and leash are presented without fanfare and donned only when the dog is calm. When visitors arrive at your door, the leader does not open the door until the dog is calm and isn't attempting to get through the door to greet the arrivals.

Precautions

When a healthy adult Boxer is comfortable and familiar with the practices of controlled walking, he is ready to join you in jogging. Boxers are good jogging partners because their size and energy level are well matched to a human's pace and stamina. The same common sense rules apply:

- Do not take your Boxer jogging on very warm days.
- Maintain control of your Boxer at all times.
- If you plan to jog on a track or trail, make sure that dogs are permitted.

- Watch your Boxer for signs of fatigue or hyperthermia.
- Provide plenty of fresh, cool water afterward.

Boxers should be at least one year old before embarking on a jogging partnership with you. Frequent jogging can damage a puppy's developing skeletal structure, and a puppy won't have the stamina of an adult dog. Just as humans are advised to consult their physician before embarking on exercise programs, a brief chat with the vet about your plans to jog with your Boxer will allay any doubts.

CANINE GOOD CITIZEN® PROGRAM

Established in 1989 by the American Kennel Club (AKC), the Canine Good Citizen (CGC) program stresses responsible pet ownership and the importance of a well-mannered dog. All breeds are eligible for the CGC title, even those yet unrecognized by the AKC, as well as mixed-breed dogs. Many Boxer owners choose the CGC program as the first step in training their dogs because it lays an excellent foundation for other standardized activities, such as therapy dog, obedience, agility, and more. Successful Canine Good Citizens are included in the AKC's database of CGC-certified dogs, and their owners receive a certificate of accomplishment. The program is popular with 4-H Clubs around the country, which use it as a beginner's dog training course for children. The CGC program has been so successful in the United States that other countries are realizing

Training Tidbit

The same safety guidelines that human athletes practice apply to canine athletes too:
- Before starting any activity, have the vet check your Boxer to make sure that he is in good health and able to safely participate in your chosen sport.
- Condition your Boxer gradually before plunging into competitive sports. A dog who doesn't properly train for an event or keep in shape between events is susceptible to injury.
- Warm up your Boxer prior to events. He should never go from the crate to the event without a brisk walk or a quick game of fetch to get his blood pumping.
- Make sure that your Boxer is hydrated before events. Excited dogs don't always bother to drink, so give him plenty of water the day before a competition. In very hot weather, avoid ice and ice water, which can cause cramps. Offer him cool water right after exercise, limiting him to the amount he can drink in one minute. Cool him down with easy walking, then offer more water.
- If your chosen activity requires your Boxer to wear anything, even just a collar and leash, make sure that it fits properly and doesn't irritate him in any way.

its value as an evaluating tool for a dog's potential.

The CGC test consists of ten sections, each involving regular, everyday occurrences with which a normal, well-behaved dog should have no trouble coping:

1. allowing a friendly stranger to approach
2. sitting calmly and politely to be petted
3. permitting handling for grooming and physical examination
4. heeling on a loose lead
5. walking calmly through crowded areas
6. sitting on command; downing on command
7. coming when called
8. greeting another obedient dog without aggression or excitement
9. coping with distractions and distracting environments
10. behaving well while under the care of another, with the owner out of sight

Owners are allowed to praise and encourage their Boxers as they perform these actions during testing but are forbidden to use toys and treats as enticements. Also prohibited are special training collars, such as prong collars, head halters, and electronic collars. Grounds for failure include aggressive behavior by the dog, elimination or marking of territory, and whining or any displays of nervousness.

Even if you have no plans to become involved in any organized dog activities, the CGC training and test is an excellent way for you to bond with your Boxer while he learns to respect your authority. Education is never wasted.

BOXER SPORTS

The Boxer's athletic build, high energy level, and playful personality make him a natural for many organized dog activities sponsored around the world by various organizations such as the International Agility Link (IAL) and the Canine Freestyle Federation, Inc. (CFF). As a working dog, the Boxer thrives on situations that challenge him mentally and physically, especially if pleasing his human is the payoff. Plus, you'll have the opportunity to meet other Boxer owners and share information in a fun environment.

Agility

The athletic Boxer is well suited to the physically demanding sport of agility, in which a coordinated, well-trained dog navigates a very intricate obstacle course of hurdles, tunnels, seesaws, and the like. Participants are timed, with contenders of exceptional drive winning the race. The sport is modeled after equine open jumping classes, in which horse and rider complete an obstacle course in the fastest time with the fewest number of faults. In canine agility, herding breeds have the instinctual advantage, but the Boxer's natural dexterity and intelligence make him a force to be reckoned with. Competition notwithstanding, a Boxer will certainly give his all to this energetic activity, and you'll both have a lot of fun in the process.

Thanks to agility's ever-growing popularity in the United States, five major

Want to Know More?

If your Boxer gets especially dirty participating in a sport or activity, he may need a full-on grooming session. See Chapter 6: Boxer Grooming Needs for some pointers.

The Boxer's athletic build, high energy level, and playful personality mean that he may enjoy a sport like agility.

organizations standardize and sponsor the sport: the AKC, Canine Performance Events (CPE), the United States Dog Agility Association, Inc. (USDAA), the United Kennel Club (UKC), and the North American Dog Agility Council (NADAC). Each offers its own titles that cannot be interchanged. In other words, even if your Boxer has earned the top agility title offered by the AKC, he must start at the bottom of CPE's program. Although most utilize the same course obstacles, there may be some that are particular to a certain organization or that have varying specifications. You can visit each group's website to learn the differences and decide which one best suits you and your Boxer.

Canine Freestyle

Derived from equine dressage class, in which horse and rider perform certain movements in sync with music, canine freestyle is a relatively new dog sport most prevalent in Canada, where it originated. Unofficially known as "dancing with dogs," freestyle is subdivided into two categories. Musical freestyle is a choreographed routine set to music, in which dog and handler perform intricate moves showcasing creativity, teamwork, athleticism, artistry, and interpretation of the accompanying music. In heelwork-to-music, the choreography is even more intricate, and dog and handler perform more synchronized movements that adhere to heelwork specifications. Heelwork is defined by the World Canine Freestyle Organization (WCFO) as any position between handler and dog within a 360-degree radius, including but not limited to right heel; left heel; face-to-face; face-to-back; back-to-back; back-to-face; and all angled positions between dog and handler within 360 degrees.

Both styles are entertaining and beautiful to watch. If you envision yourself dancing with a Boxer, any of the major freestyle organizations can help educate you on the sport: the CFF, Inc., the WCFO, and the Musical Dog Sports Association (MDSA).

Conformation

Conformation refers to a competition in which each entrant is evaluated against his most current published breed standard. Although not a "sport" in the strictest sense of the word, conformation requires that carefully bred and trained dogs meet exacting requirements in the show ring. Unlike other activities, where a dog's athleticism and dexterity determine his success, conformation emphasizes appearance and temperament. Those unfamiliar with conformation may consider it nothing more than a canine beauty pageant, but the sport has a bona fide purpose as a showcase for breeding stock to preserve breed integrity. Looks definitely play an important part, but the ultimate goal is the ongoing improvement of the breed.

If conformation is your chosen activity, learn as much as you can about the Boxer breed, and study conformation structure and operation before acquiring a dog. The next step is to find a reputable Boxer breeder who can not only sell you a puppy with show potential, but can provide you with information resources to start you on your way. Conformation shows are offered by a variety of kennel clubs, large and small, often with varying breed classifications and prestige factors. Finding those that align

The sensitive Boxer is a perfect candidate for therapy work.

During a conformation event, the dog is judged against the standard for his breed.

with your goals is your best chance for conformation success.

Obedience

Competitive obedience is more than just flaunting how easily your Boxer performs the basic commands. Originating in the 1930s, this sport demonstrates a dog's utility as a companion to mankind. Dog and handler are judged as a team on how closely they match the judge's idea of perfectly executed exercises. Obedience competition showcases the handler's training ability and the dog's willingness to perform on command, so a handler's natural movement and the dog's demeanor are crucial to the judging process. Points are awarded for successful completion of specific moves required in individual classes that increase in difficulty. Each level of obedience skill must be mastered before advancing to the next. Most obedience titles are awarded after earning three qualifying scores ("legs") in the appropriate class, under three different judges.

The Boxer's natural desire to please his human makes him a good candidate for obedience competition. If you're interested in competing in obedience, contact one of the sponsors, like the AKC, for information to get you started

Schützhund

Schützhund is German for "protection dog," so what better activity for a working dog like the Boxer? Originally developed to test the mettle of the German Shepherd Dog,

Schützhund resembles agility and obedience but is distinguished by its focus on the development of protective traits, and is a test of a dog's ability to follow directions. Schützhund competition measures a dog's mental stability, stamina, tracking ability, gameness, structural efficiency, and trainability.

Schützhund trials include a test in which the dog attacks the owner/handler's arm while it is sheathed in a thick, protective burlap sleeve. It is important to understand that Schützhund does not promote aggression in a dog's temperament; it is just another sport that demonstrates a dog's obedience and utility. A dog participating in Schützhund is trained not to bite anything but the burlap sleeve. Advanced-level titles are awarded to dogs who master difficult scent-tracking trials and guardian tests. Not surprisingly, many law enforcement personnel and their dogs are attracted to Schützhund, but "civilian" families equally enjoy the sport.

THERAPY WORK

No one knows better than a Boxer fancier that having a pet is therapeutic. It's been scientifically proven that petting a dog can lower blood pressure and reduce stress. When we're not feeling quite right, the sensitive Boxer knows that a hug and a few kisses are in order, making the breed a perfect fit for therapy work.

Therapy dogs visit hospitals, special-needs facilities, schools, and nursing homes, interacting with patients and residents, sharing their endless natural love of people. Therapy work carries the added bonus of diffusing any misconceptions that Boxers are aggressive or vicious. Their endearing enthusiasm, however, may be overwhelming in a clinical setting, so Boxers should acquire their CGC certification before embarking on therapy work. In fact, although the organizations that train and provide therapy dog services may have their own requirements, CGC is usually an applicant's basic credential.

TRAVELING WITH YOUR BOXER

Once upon a time, families used to pile into their station wagons and take off, blissfully ignorant of future safety features like air bags and seat belts. We know better now.

Your Boxer will sometimes need to travel—starting with his first trip home with you—across town, or across the country. Dogs involved in organized sports or activities often travel far and wide for events, and many dog owners vacation only where their dogs are also welcome. Every mode of transportation has its own safety concerns, but with the right information and planning, your Boxer can safely and comfortably travel with or without you.

Car Travel

Your dog's security in the car is as important as any passenger's. A responsible owner

By the Numbers

Although most organized dog activities involve adolescent or adult dogs, a Boxer puppy as young as 10 to 12 weeks can begin training for conformation.

Your Boxer should never be left in a parked car, even with the windows open.

makes certain that her Boxer is comfortably restrained with a dog safety harness or inside a crate that has been firmly anchored inside the car. Most safety harnesses allow the dog to lie down on the seat while maintaining sufficient restraint in the event of an accident or short stop. Aside from the obvious safety benefits, restraints prevent your Boxer from suddenly jumping up or otherwise disrupting your control of the vehicle.

In addition to a crate or safety harness for a motor trip, remember to take these essentials along for your traveling pooch:

- extra leash and collar with duplicate ID tags
- sufficient food and water for the trip and destination
- favorite blanket or bed to throw in the crate or seat for extra comfort
- chew toys to keep him occupied during vacation downtime
- waste removal bags—a must no matter where you travel
- important documentation: identification registry phone numbers, health certificates, local veterinary information
- towels to clean dirty paws, etc.
- first-aid kit with disinfectant, gauze pads or cotton balls, anti-nausea medication, tweezers for tick removal, antihistamine for insect stings, self-adhesive roll bandage

Car travel with your Boxer has a few important caveats:

- Never allow your Boxer to ride unrestrained in an open truck bed. Not only is it illegal in some areas, but it is foolishly risky. An abrupt stop can send him tumbling around the truck bed or out into traffic. He may also see something irresistible and jump out, even if the truck is moving.

- Never let your Boxer hold his head out of a moving car's open window. Flying debris can cause serious injury to his eyes and ears.

- Never leave your Boxer in a parked car, even with the windows open. In warm weather, a closed car heats up like a greenhouse in a very short time and will cause heatstroke, a particular bane of the short-nosed Boxer. Even if the outside temperature is mild and pleasant, the car's interior can heat up to a dangerous level, and open windows don't ventilate sufficiently. Neither should you leave a pet in the car with the air-conditioning running while you pop into a store or take a restroom break. To do so requires you to leave the keys in the car, an open invitation to steal the dog, the car, or both.

We live in an era when no crime is unthinkable. No longer is a lost dog the worst possibility we can imagine.

If you are traveling with your Boxer, make sure he's well trained.

Unsupervised dogs are often stolen for nefarious purposes: used as "bait" dogs in illegal dog-fight training (Boxers are particular targets because of their gameness and strength), sold to science laboratories as experiment subjects, or sold anywhere to anyone, just to make a quick buck. Do not assume that your Boxer is safe anywhere without some kind of security or supervision.

Air Travel

Air travel may well be a journeying Boxer's only transportation option because dogs (with the exception of assistance dogs) are not permitted on commercial trains or buses, and driving has limitations. Commercial airlines will permit small pets in the passenger cabin if their carriers are small enough to fit underneath your seat. Only a young Boxer puppy meets that requirement. If you plan to fly your Boxer, thoroughly research the airlines' policies on dog transport, required documentation (health certificates and identification), and quarantine laws, if applicable. Be sure to ask for all costs applying to pet travel, as well as the airline's procedures for loading and unloading live animals.

Because large companion animals are typically carried in the belly of most commercial airplanes, air transport comes with safety issues. Fortunately, contemporary airlines have much more stringent regulations regarding the carriage of animals than ever before, considerably reducing risk. Time of year, time of day, length of flight, service routes, weather at origin and destination, and the number of animals flying are all factors in safe air carriage, and each airline has its own set of restrictions, as well as acceptable crate types. Consequently, careful planning is imperative.

Despite precautions, air travel can be stressful for dogs, even seasoned travelers. The deafening noise, huge moving objects, bustling atmosphere, and unfamiliar surroundings are frightening for a dog about to travel by plane. Historically, veterinarians have prescribed sedatives for dogs on airplanes, but some experts believe that the decreased heart and respiration rates caused by sedation are more dangerous than the actual stressors of flying. If your Boxer must travel by air, discuss sedation with your vet to decide what is best for your dog.

Lodging for Humans and Pets

Pet-friendly lodgings are springing up everywhere, attesting to our dogs' firmly entrenched position as members of the family. Hotels that welcome dogs often require a small deposit against any damages. Sometimes this deposit is nonrefundable and used to deodorize and thoroughly clean the lodging for the next guests and their pets. Play by the rules and don't smuggle your dog (although it's hard to smuggle a full-grown Boxer anywhere!) into lodgings with a no-pets policy. If the housekeeping staff isn't aware that the room needs special cleaning, a future guest with an allergy could suffer. Nor should you leave your Boxer in the car all night while you sleep in the hotel. It will either be too cold or too hot, and there is always the risk of theft, not to mention your Boxer's unhappiness at the inexplicable separation from his humans.

Multi-Dog Tip

If more than one Boxer will be traveling by air, make sure that the airline understands that they are traveling together. The number of live animals carried on a flight is usually limited, and you don't want your dogs inadvertently separated because the airline overlooked a prior reservation for another dog.

If you can't travel with your Boxer, doggy day care is one option.

An Internet search can quickly give you information on pet-friendly accommodations along your travel route. The best resources for up-to-date listings of pet-friendly lodging are websites like www.pettravel.us and www.dogfriendly.com. Travel agencies and the American Automobile Association (AAA) may also help. When in doubt, call a hotel directly to inquire about its pet policies. If the hotel doesn't accept dogs, it might tell you of a nearby hotel that does. Some have weight or size restrictions or only accept cats, so verify that a Boxer meets the hotels requirements. When you and your Boxer avail yourselves of pet-friendly accommodations, remember that you are ambassadors for all travelers with pets. Impeccable guest conduct will inspire hotels and motels to continue to welcome pets.

When You Can't Take Your Boxer With You

One of the most important considerations when acquiring a dog is the question of who will take care of your pet when you cannot. Even if you plan to include your dog in all vacations and activities, a time will come when you simply cannot take him along. Fortunately, several options exist to care for your Boxer and give you peace of mind.

Doggy Day Care

As the name implies, doggy day care is an organized program/facility that cares for your dog during working hours. Similar to human child day care programs, doggy day care provides supervision, socialization, and activity for one or more dogs. They do not accept clients on a walk-in basis; potential client dogs must apply and are approved after demonstrating an affable temperament with caregivers and other dogs. Because Boxers can be dog-aggressive, this application process is justified. Day care programs typically do not offer overnight care and therefore may not be the best choice if you plan to travel out of town. Sometimes, day care providers develop relationships with their clients that progress to vacation care, but it should not be expected.

In-Home Pet Sitting

Professional pet sitting is a booming business, responding to an ever-growing demand for pets to be cared for in the comfort and familiarity of their own homes. Pet sitters typically visit the home one or more times a day to feed and exercise the pet, as well as administer any medications. Even better is the sitter who will live in your home during your absence. Your Boxer has the benefit of companionship, and you are assured of his safety in the event of a health or household emergency. You also have someone to take in your mail, water your plants, and ensure the safety of your home.

Before you allow a stranger access to your dog and your home, find out if the sitter is fully bonded and insured. Ask for references. Better yet, get a referral from another dog owner whose judgment you trust. Invite the sitter to come over and meet your pet while you are present. How does she interact with the dog? Is she experienced with Boxers? Does she have a stand-by person in place, in case she is unable to get to your dog? Both you and your dog should feel comfortable being with this person, and vice versa.

Boarding Kennels

A good boarding kennel can be a perfectly acceptable situation for your Boxer in your absence. Many dogs enjoy the camaraderie of other boarders and the attention of friendly caregivers. Boarding kennels vary from basic indoor/outdoor cement runs to plush puppy palaces, complete with spa treatments. Most animal hospitals and veterinary practices also offer boarding services to their clients. Before you leave your Boxer anywhere for the first time, pay a visit together to the kennel. Are the boarding and exercise areas clean and comfortable? Is water always accessible? How much personal, individual attention will your dog receive? Is someone on the premises 24/7?

Boarding kennels typically require proof of vaccination currency, as well as vaccination against kennel cough. They encourage you to bring a supply of the food your dog eats at home to prevent digestive upset. A favorite toy and blanket go a long way toward making a boarder feel more comfortable while his humans are away.

PART III

SENIOR YEARS

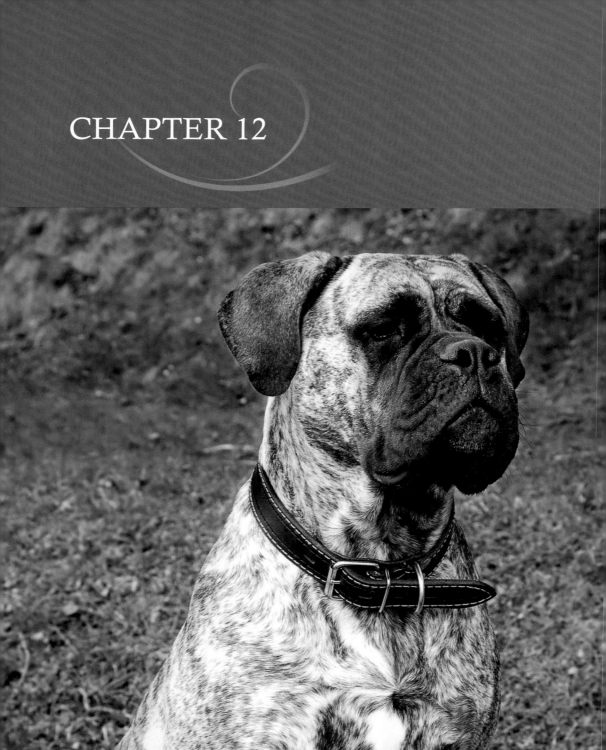

CHAPTER 12

FINDING YOUR SENIOR BOXER

Large dog breeds generally have shorter life spans than small breeds. A Boxer is considered fully mature between 18 and 24 months of age, and a geriatric—or "silver"—Boxer at 7 or 8 years. But don't expect to see him slow down just because he's officially a senior citizen. His pep and playfulness will seem paradoxical to the gray or white hairs appearing on his muzzle. As his hair changes increasingly to gray, his face will take on a silvery appearance, hence the euphemism "silver Boxer."

WHY OLDER DOGS NEED NEW HOMES

Why would older dogs need new homes? Sadly, in most cases, they simply weren't wanted anymore. An unfortunate truth is that some heartless dog owners view pets as disposable. Lack of commitment to an older dog who develops physical limitations, is no longer "fun," or who can't be relocated with his family results in geriatric pets dumped at shelters, where they will languish until euthanized for lack of space—or worse, to older dogs abandoned outside to fend for themselves. Sometimes even well-loved senior dogs become homeless when their owners die suddenly or without custody arrangements. Whatever the reason, a homeless senior dog will not live out his days with the love and comfort he deserves unless adopted.

THE CONS OF SENIOR DOG ADOPTION

Adopting a geriatric dog is not for everyone. The inevitable issues that come with old age may be too burdensome. If he doesn't have any medical issues yet, the chances of developing one during the remainder of his life are reasonable. He may have emotional and/or physical problems that require more care and accommodation than would a younger dog. His span of time with you as a family member will obviously be shorter than a puppy or young adult's. And let's face it: An adorable puppy or adolescent with personality is more likely to be adopted than a stately senior.

Want to Know More?

If adopting an adult is more to your liking, see Chapter 5: Finding Your Adult Boxer.

Older Boxers' coats begin to turn gray as they age.

A Boxer is considered a senior at age seven or eight. Elderly Boxers may experience a gradual deterioration in the acuity of the five senses, with his sense of smell the last to decline.

THE PROS OF SENIOR DOG ADOPTION

On the other hand, the benefits of adopting an older dog can't be denied. Older dogs are usually comfortable with the basic components of daily life that you must gradually train a puppy to accept: the crate, car rides, leash walking, temporary separations, and toileting. Homeless seniors are especially grateful to be adopted and typically bond quickly to their new family, with a shorter adjustment phase. Senior dogs usually don't have the frenetic energy that they did in their prime, which translates into quiet, loving company at your feet (or if Boxers have their way, in your lap) while you watch television or work at the computer. An older dog's physical and mental development is complete; you

Multi-Dog Tip

Allow each dog in your pack to have his own crate. Even the best of canine friends need space and time apart from one another in a private refuge.

shouldn't encounter any appearance or behavior surprises.

WHERE TO FIND SENIOR DOGS TO ADOPT

Where do you find older dogs available for adoption? Most local animal shelters have a number of them, but there's no guarantee that they will have a Boxer. Breeders sometimes have older dogs to rehome, especially if adult Boxers they have sold as pets were returned to the breeder for whatever reason. Boxer rescue organizations are the richest source of adoptable seniors; some even specialize in silver Boxers, recognizing the need for a community in which homeless seniors don't end their lives in shelter cages or pens, watching the puppies and young adults find adoptive homes. Silver Boxer rescue can also provide support if you're inexperienced with silver Boxers and the physical debilitations that typically afflict older dogs: incontinence, arthritis, cataracts, etc.

Yes, adopting an older Boxer means fewer years together before facing the inevitable loss. But don't let that keep you from considering adoption of an older dog. No matter how long or short the time, you are gifting him with security, love, and peace as he ends his days. Adopting an older dog is an act of kindness that will enrich your life as much as it will his.

CHAPTER 13

CARE OF YOUR SENIOR BOXER

When your Boxer is in the prime of life, it's easy to think that he'll go on forever. But the silver and white hairs starting to dust his muzzle by age seven or eight remind us that, although his zest for life is unchanged, his body is changing. Modern medicine has enabled our pets to enjoy a longer life with us, but owners are still responsible for taking the necessary steps to keep them comfortable and healthy during the silver years: the right food, exercise, and awareness of any behavioral deviances that could indicate a potential health problem.

THE SIGNS OF AGING

Silver hairs are not the only evidence that your Boxer is getting on in years. In fact, an aging Boxer undergoes many of the same physical changes that aging humans experience: a decrease in stamina, increased need for sleep, digestive upsets, and the development of degenerative conditions like arthritis and cataracts. Ongoing observation of your Boxer will alert you to most signs of aging.

Weight Gain

An older Boxer may gain a few pounds (kg) even though he is not eating any more than his usual quantities—a definite sign of a slowing metabolism. Excess weight is no better for an older Boxer than it is for an older human. Extra pounds (kg) can increase stress on the heart and on joints that may already be bothersome due to arthritis. To combat unhealthy weight gain, continue walking and exercising your silver Boxer. He may no longer beg you for a walk by wriggling next to the place where his leash is kept and fixing you with those hopeful eyes, so it's up to you to maintain his walking schedule. Even if he doesn't initiate the idea, a healthy older Boxer should always gladly accompany his human on a casual walk. If you notice a reluctance to walk or difficulty standing, sitting, or lying down, painful arthritis may be to blame. Consult your vet about medication to alleviate his discomfort.

Another way to challenge a retarded metabolism is to reduce the amount of food your dog eats. If his appetite seems unsatisfied with smaller portions, talk to

An aging Boxer undergoes many of the same physical changes that aging humans experience.

your vet about changing to a different food, one formulated for overweight dogs. It's important to maintain a proper protein content in the senior dog's diet, especially if he suffers from kidney problems.

Weight gain is not always a by-product of an aging metabolism, however. It can also be a symptom of health issues like hypothyroidism, a dysfunction of the thyroid gland. Be sure to have the vet rule out any medical conditions that might cause unusual weight gain.

Oral Problems

Oral care for aging Boxers is important because many develop gingival hyperplasia, an overgrowth of gum tissue that envelops teeth and affects proper bite. The pockets of moist, warm tissue are hospitable to bacteria that can cause bad breath or infection. If hyperplasia starts to interfere with a dog's eating ability, veterinary excision may be required. The tissues are merely snipped away, without sutures and with very little bleeding. There is minimal pain afterward, although soft foods are advised for a few days. Because dogs won't hold still for such a procedure, it must be done under general anesthesia, which carries an inherent risk for even the healthiest of patients, human or canine. This risk increases with a patient's age, so Boxers with significant cases of gingival hyperplasia should undergo the procedure sooner rather than later. Many vets recommend taking advantage of the dog's anesthetized state to perform a full dental cleaning.Dental instruments remove plaque from less accessible places, like the gum line and the rear molars, and the teeth are thoroughly examined for decay or other problems. Although the risk of complications from anesthesia increases proportionately with the length of time a patient is under anesthesia, the extra time incurred by a dental cleaning should not contribute significantly. Be sure to talk to your vet about any concerns you may have.

Incontinence

Urinary incontinence (the inability to control urination) is a common by-product of aging, particularly in spayed middle-aged females.

You may start to notice leaking while your Boxer is relaxed or sleeping. Incontinence can have a variety of causes, so before attributing it to aging, you must rule out other possibilities. The vet will test a urine sample and take a thorough history of the dog's urinary tract: reproductive ability, age at spaying/neutering, age at incontinence onset, frequency of occurrence, amount of passed urine, the dog's own awareness of leakage, etc. If a urinalysis reveals the presence of mineral crystals in the dog's urine, he may have a pH imbalance. Crystals are often the precursor to bladder or kidney stones, which can cause painful urination and serious illness. A special food with a higher acid content is usually prescribed to restore a proper pH balance. If urinalysis and culture do not reveal infection,

A senior dog can make a wonderful pet.

but the urine is more dilute than it should be, the vet will submit a blood sample to test for kidney or other organic disease that can affect urine's normal concentration, such as Cushing's disease and diabetes. If tests rule out a more serious health issue, age-related incontinence can be controlled with medication or contained by using special "panties" with pads designed for canine incontinence and estrus.

FEEDING

The older dog's nutritional needs are essentially no different from his younger counterpart, but he may have different circumstances that require attention to his diet.

Maintain Proper Protein Levels

A widely held belief was that senior dogs don't require as much protein as in their prime adult years, and that maintaining adult protein levels in a healthy senior dog's food would foster kidney problems. Studies have refuted this theory, revealing that a senior dog's diet should have optimal protein content to maintain good health.

Maintain Proper Fat Levels

Similarly, it's important to maintain a proper level of fat in a senior's diet. An overweight Boxer can and should eat a reduced-fat diet, but the reduction should be proportional, as part of an overall lower-calorie plan. If fat intake is severely reduced, his skin may develop an uncomfortable itch. His coat may appear lackluster, with dandruff. Without sufficient fat stores in his body, he may become easily chilled. If any dietary modification becomes necessary, it is best altered under a vet's supervision to ensure that your senior's nutritional needs continue to be met.

Make sure that your senior Boxer's is food highly digestible to accommodate his digestive tract.

Make the Food More Digestible

A silver Boxer's food should be highly digestible to accommodate a digestive tract that may become sluggish, and it must be tasty enough to ensure that he'll eat it. A senior dog whose appetite becomes uncharacteristically finicky may have an underlying issue. Sometimes older dogs experience tooth or gum sensitivity that can make eating uncomfortable. If the vet discerns that no significant teeth or gum problems are contributing to this change in eating habits, switching to softer foods may help.

Warm the Food

A decreased sense of smell can also contribute to a senior's decreased or finicky appetite. You can make his food more tempting by warming it slightly (ensuring that it's not hot enough to burn his mouth or tongue) to increase the aroma and stimulate the appetite. You can also tempt him by stirring in some low-sodium chicken broth, unsweetened applesauce, or the drained, flavorful water in which canned vegetables and tuna are packed.

Add Fiber

Senior dogs who experience temporary constipation often find relief in diets with added fiber. Increasing your dog's daily fiber intake to 3 to 5 percent should help common constipation issues and keep him feeling fuller longer. Mixing a tablespoon or two of wheat or oat bran into his food is a convenient way to add fiber without altering the taste. You can also offer him raw mini

The low-maintenance Boxer is a clean dog who often grooms himself like a cat.

carrots and apple slices, both good sources of fiber that many dogs consider special treats.

Nutritional Supplements

Nutritional supplements for older dogs are popular for issues like dry skin and painful joints. Some dog owners feel their seniors can benefit from the addition of antioxidants for overall health. Supplements are an easy way to provide your Boxer with any additional vitamins and minerals he may need, but *only* under a vet's supervision. Don't assume that the same supplements and dosages we take ourselves are appropriate to give your Boxer. It is very easy to accidentally overdose nutritional supplements and create physical problems where there were none. If your silver Boxer has a problem like arthritis, and you want to try supplementing his diet with glucosamine and chondroitin (thought to aid in cartilage regeneration), talk to your vet about proper dosage and formulas.

Want to Know More?

For a refresher on detailed grooming techniques, see Chapter 6: Boxer Grooming Needs.

When and How Often to Feed

When and how often to feed your silver Boxer is really based on your best judgment and your dog's habits. Most dogs eat twice a day throughout their adult lives, typically including a morning meal to fuel their metabolism for the day. If your schedule takes you out of the house in the morning, offer your dog's breakfast with plenty of time for elimination before you leave. A second meal offered in the late afternoon or early evening will satisfy hunger and allow plenty of time for digestion between meals. If you find that your older Boxer thrives on a three-meal schedule, be sure to portion the correct amount of food among the three meals, rather than adding an extra portion with the third feeding.

GROOMING

The low-maintenance Boxer is a very clean dog who often grooms himself like a cat. His short coat doesn't become matted or retain dirt the way a longer-coated breed might. As he ages, though, he may need a little extra help from you.

Skin and Coat

With age, perhaps the most noticeable changes we humans undergo are visible on our skin. Silver Boxers can similarly experience many of these changes. Their skin may become dry and sensitive, with or without dandruff. A senior dog experiencing mental changes associated with aging may lose interest in previously fastidious self-grooming habits. Hormonal imbalances can also affect the skin, making it thin, fragile, and slow to heal. Light-colored skin can become darker and thicker in appearance, sometimes mottled. New lumps and bumps may appear, especially in Boxers, who are so prone to skin tumors in general. As with any significant change in your dog's appearance and behavior, have the vet ascertain if an underlying medical issue may be a factor. If not, she can then explain the changes in your senior's skin and coat, and recommend any helpful action, if necessary.

Nails

The toenails become thicker and more brittle with age, which can make trimming more difficult. Senior dogs sometimes develop a dislike of having their paws handled, further complicating the procedure. It's important to keep up a nail trimming regimen to prevent any impediment to comfortable walking or potential injury. The longer the nail is allowed to grow past its customary length, the longer the quick also grows, meaning that you must cut the quick to restore the previous length. No dog likes that, senior or otherwise. Maintaining a nail trimming routine with a reluctant senior dog is still easier than becoming lax about this important grooming chore and dealing with the ensuing repercussions.

Arthritis

You have probably noticed over the years that your Boxer often groomed his own nether regions. But a silver Boxer with arthritis may lose the flexibility to comfortably assume the acrobatic poses necessary to accomplish the task. A box of flushable baby wipes is handy for post-toileting cleanup, as well as for removing any mud or dirt on the underbelly acquired during an outside excursion. They work well on dirty paws too, especially between the toes.

Alternatively, a washcloth dampened with warm water will accomplish the same task.

How to Groom the Silver Boxer

Boxers continue to shed their fur throughout their lives, so even senior citizens without any skin issues still need regular brushing. Using a soft bristle brush with gentle strokes in the same direction as the hair grows will keep his silver coat looking as dashing as ever.

Regular vet checkups are essential to preserving your Boxer's good health and quality of life.

It's helpful to be aware of the conditions that can afflict your Boxer and their symptoms so that you can better expedite diagnosis and treatment.

If your Boxer has trouble standing or sitting for a brushing, take advantage of his relaxed moments to brush him. If he's napping on his side, gently pet him to alert him to your presence, then softly brush as much area as you can, taking extra care on any sensitive spots he may have. Later, when he changes position, brush those exposed areas. Just as in his younger days, your silver Boxer will enjoy the petting sensation that grooming mimics.

If your senior Boxer needs a bath, make certain that the room is warm enough before wetting him. Place a nonskid rubber mat on the bottom of the tub to give him the security of firm footing. Do not allow or encourage him to jump into the tub. Instead, carefully lift him by placing one arm around the front of his chest near the legs and the other arm behind his back legs, underneath the rump. This will alleviate the pressure on the rib cage that results when you lift him with both arms underneath his body. Gently place him in the tub and remove your arms only when you are sure of his footing and balance. Bathe as usual, using an extra-mild dog shampoo.

When grooming your silver Boxer, don't forget to include his eyes and ears. This is a good time to look for any cloudiness or secretion in his eyes, and to make sure that his ears are clean and odor-free.

HEALTH CARE

Regular veterinary checkups are essential to preserving your silver Boxer's good health and quality of life. In addition to yearly blood tests for heartworm, yearly analyses of stool and urine samples are a good way to make sure that no underlying infections, parasites, or metabolic issues need to be addressed. Annual veterinary exams should also detect any abnormalities in heart or lung function, as well as skin tumors or cysts.

Certain medical conditions tend to prevail in some breeds more so than others. Some ailments tend to afflict older dogs more than puppies and young adults. Some illnesses do both. It's helpful to be aware of these conditions and their symptoms in order to expedite diagnosis and treatment.

Arthritis

As common among senior dogs as it is among senior humans, "arthritis" literally means "joint inflammation." Arthritis is not just one disease; it's an umbrella term for over 100 types of joint disorders that afflict mostly elderly canines and humans, but are not age-exclusive. The most common form is osteoarthritis (OA), in which the cartilage (the cushioning substance that prevents bones from rubbing directly against one another and causing severe pain) loses elasticity and damages easily, wearing thin or even tearing.

OA (also known as degenerative joint disease or DJD) afflicts many dogs, primarily middle-aged to geriatric dogs, although it can also occur in young dogs suffering from hip dysplasia. In most cases, OA occurs in the aftermath of an injury, nutritional disorders, or infection. A broken bone may be set and heal properly, but the trauma leaves it more susceptible to the onset of arthritis. Untreated, arthritis can cause pain, impair mobility, and continue to degenerate.

Drug therapy is used to control the pain of arthritis, maximize mobility, retard the destructive process occurring in the joint, and encourage cartilage repair. Nonsteroidal anti-inflammatory drugs (NSAIDs), such as aspirin, are the most commonly used medication. NSAIDs are widely successfully in alleviating the symptoms of arthritis but can have side effects, such as stomach ulcers and bleeding. Another popular treatment modality employs chondroprotective agents that help regenerate cartilage. Because the two drug types work in different ways, they can be taken simultaneously to combat the pain and progression of arthritis. Consult your vet before administering any over-the-counter medicines to your dog. If pain management is ineffective, surgery may be an option to realign or replace joints. Acupuncture, an alternative treatment not scientifically proven to

Multi-Dog Tip

If you are planning to adopt a new puppy but already own a geriatric dog, consider how the new arrival may affect the established pet. Senior dogs don't always tolerate the antics of puppies, or they may develop territorial behavior. Consult your vet or breeder about the possible repercussions of introducing a puppy into a senior's world.

Just like any breed, Boxers can suffer from a variety of illnesses as they age.

manage pain when drug therapy failed, has been reported by some dog owners to reduce arthritis discomfort. Keeping the dog motionless while acupuncture needles are inserted sometimes presents a challenge, however.

Canine Cognitive Dysfunction Syndrome

Canine cognitive dysfunction syndrome (CDS) is a sad affliction marked by a decline in a dog's cognitive abilities, similar to dementia in humans. It is caused by physical and chemical changes in the brain of an older dog, usually in the final trimester of life. This degenerative condition comes on slowly and may cause discomfort or behavioral changes. Sight, hearing, smell, and taste may be reduced, and spatial orientation may be affected. An affected dog might wander aimlessly, appear confused, have a glazed expression, and/or regress in housetraining habits. His personality may seem more aloof or guarded, especially if he has difficulty recognizing family members. Uncharacteristic personality changes can appear, such as formerly timid dogs becoming aggressive, or elderly dogs may develop obsessive activities, like licking. Other symptoms include increased diurnal sleep and decreased nocturnal sleep, possibly with barking for no apparent reason.

Before diagnosing CDS, the vet will rule out other diseases with similar symptoms. If CDS is responsible for a dog's unusual behavior, drug therapy to enhance the activity of a brain chemical called dopamine may help cognitive function. Side effects like vomiting and diarrhea, although rare, can occur. Your vet may recommend nutritional supplements like omega-3 fatty acids, vitamin C, and beta-carotene, known to contribute to enhanced brain function. She may also encourage more activity that requires the dog to think, which can help improve his overall behavior. Playing with other pets or with toys that dispense treats when the dog performs certain actions are helpful to dogs with CDS. Taking him out of his comfort zone of home and into new situations can also boost cognitive ability.

Congestive Heart Failure

Congestive heart failure (CHF) occurs when the heart can no longer pump blood to the lungs and/or body at the proper volume and pressure. If the heart's blood output is decreased, the relative amount of blood input is increased. This altered balance of fluid pressures causes blood fluids to leave the vessels and congest surrounding tissues. The heart ultimately fails, causing death. There is no cure. The two most common causes of CHF in dogs are degenerative valvular disease (DVD) and dilated cardiomyopathy (DCM), a particular bane of Boxers.

DVD reduces the ability of the heart valves to prevent backflow of blood during ventricular contraction. The valve most commonly involved is the mitral or left atrial-ventricular valve. In these cases, the condition is called mitral valve disease (MVD).

DCM is a progressive enlargement of the chamber inside the heart's ventricle, with a steady weakening of ventricular contractions. The disease is characterized by two distinct phases: a subclinical or occult phase, and the overt clinical phase. In the occult phase, there are no outward clinical signs of heart disease even though dysfunction is taking place. Often the disease is undetected until the affected dog progresses to the overt clinical phase and symptoms appear, including coughing, fainting, fatigue, decreased appetite, and difficulty sleeping (especially on the dog's side). Diagnostic tools include medical history, listening for heart arrhythmia, electrocardiogram, echocardiogram, and blood chemistry profile. An audible heart murmur is usually present, especially in cases of MVD. Treatment for conditions leading to CHF aims to control and relieve symptoms; there is no surgical remedy.

Veterinary science has been working hard to determine if cardiomyopathy is inherited. A genetic test is commercially available, although not yet accepted as the definitive test. Additional diagnostic methods are important for accuracy.

By the Numbers

Over half of dogs over the age of eight suffer from some form of Canine Cognitive Dysfunction Syndrome (CDS).

Cataracts

One of the most common canine eye afflictions, cataracts form due to a loss of transparency of the lens, thus reducing vision. Cataracts can be inherited or caused by infection, trauma, diabetes, or merely as a consequence of aging. If left untreated, blindness and inflammation will result, requiring daily applications of anti-inflammatory eye drops for the rest of the dog's life.

Fortunately, surgery has become widely successful as a treatment for cataracts. The affected lens is removed and replaced with an artificial lens. The cataract should be removed as soon as possible to avoid complications like retinal detachment and glaucoma. Dogs with advanced-stage cataracts may not be good candidates for surgical treatment.

Cushing's Disease

Officially known as hyperadrenocorticism, Cushing's disease is a condition resulting from the overproduction of glucocorticoid, a steroid produced by the adrenal gland that affects metabolism of carbohydrates, and to a lesser extent, fats and proteins. It usually affects dogs of middle or older age, and doesn't seem to afflict any particular breeds

The relaxed demeanor of older dogs makes them highly suitable for therapy work.

Cushing's disease usually affects dogs of middle or older age.

over others. Symptoms include increased drinking and urination, increased appetite, an enlarged abdomen from shifting fat and weakened muscle mass, hair loss, and thinning skin.

The disease has two distinct forms: pituitary dependent hyperadrenocorticism (PDH) and adrenal-based hyperadrenocorticism. The PDH form involves oversecretion of the hormone ACTH by the pituitary gland, usually because of a pituitary tumor. This form of the disease is responsible for about 80 percent of cases of Cushing's disease in dogs. The adrenal-based form typically results from a tumor on the adrenal gland, causing an oversecretion of glucocorticoid.

The first step to diagnosing Cushing's disease is a complete blood count, blood chemistry panel, and urinalysis performed during the evaluation. If these tests present abnormalities, more definitive testing can pinpoint Cushing's; however, a diagnosis should not be made solely on the basis of lab tests. A dog suspected of having the disease should present symptoms and have a medical history consistent with the diagnosis.

Treatment for Cushing's disease varies. Because a majority of cases are of the pituitary type, and because both the adrenal and pituitary forms will respond well to drug therapy, vets often don't test to discern which gland is the culprit. If an adrenal tumor is

He may slow down a bit, but your older Boxer will still enjoy playing with you.

identified as the cause, surgical removal of the tumor is an option. Surgery for pituitary tumors is usually not performed in veterinary medicine.

TRAINING

In many ways, training an older dog is easier than training a puppy. Mature dogs are not busily exploring the wonders hiding around every corner of a puppy's new world. A senior is more settled, with a longer attention span. If he's had a home with humans before, he probably understands at least the word "no." He understands dominance and pack hierarchy, and is ready and willing to follow your lead. If housetraining is on the agenda, his bladder and bowel control surpass a puppy's, provided he doesn't have any age-related incontinence. Training him in the routine of your home and authority is usually faster than with a puppy.

A senior Boxer with trauma in his history and/or behavior issues requires special handling. If you're considering adoption of a shelter or rescue Boxer, evaluate your lifestyle. Training a dog who may have problem behaviors takes extra patience and a calm environment. If your family includes young children whose energetic behavior might distract or frighten an older dog with a past, you might want to reconsider adopting an older dog. If your senior isn't familiar with basic commands or isn't crate trained, you can teach him these things just as you would a puppy: gradually, and with patience and positive reinforcement.

Just because a dog is a senior citizen doesn't mean that he can't enjoy new activities and thrive in training for them. The relaxed demeanor of older dogs makes them highly suitable for therapy work, and a senior Boxer's enjoyment of your company makes you both a good team for organized activities like tracking and obedience.

If you're adopting a geriatric dog with bad habits, like begging at the table or inappropriate barking, he can unlearn them

Training Tidbit

If you adopt an older dog who needs comprehensive training, consider a method you may not have used before, like clicker training. Enroll in a class, and learn alongside your dog. It's a nice bonding experience, and the mental stimulation will help keep his brain sharp.

through training in acceptable behaviors. It doesn't take mature dogs very long to ascertain what pleases you, and pleasing you makes Boxers happy at *any* life stage.

CHAPTER 14

END-OF-LIFE ISSUES

No one likes to think about the death of a loved one, and we spend much of our lives ignoring the idea. Funeral plans don't always include conversations on important issues like mental and physical incapacitation, quality of life, resuscitation, and pain management. Loved ones must then make decisions in an emotional, unclear state of mind, hoping that they are doing right by the patient.

Now imagine the responsibility of evaluating the quality of an ill or aged family member's life and making the decision to end it without the ability to ascertain the patient's opinion. Pet owners shoulder that burden every day.

EUTHANASIA

Medical science and public awareness have extended the life expectancy of domestic animals, but have not equally reduced the likelihood of developing incurable illnesses or conditions. Except for the minority of pets lucky enough to die peacefully in their sleep, most owners will one day face the issue of euthanasia.

Literally translated from Greek as "good death," euthanasia refers to the practice of ending another's life in a painless manner, to relieve suffering. Although in humans the practice is illegal, and in many cases, morally unacceptable, euthanasia is regularly and compassionately performed on animals suffering from uncontrollable pain or illness.

Euthanasia is typically accomplished by first administering a sedative/hypnotic drug intravenously to relax the pet and induce sleep, unaware of his surroundings and events. Sometimes called "twilight sedation," it is comparable to the relaxing effect of nitrous oxide at the dentist's office or the deep level

◯ *Training Tidbit*

The deep bond forged between you and your silver Boxer during a lifetime of positive training will facilitate your assessment of his quality of life when age and/or illness take its toll. His unwavering trust in your judgment and love will help with those difficult decisions dog owners must often make.

It's important to prepare for the passing of your older Boxer.

of sedation administered prior to medical procedures like colonoscopy. When the vet is confident of the dog's anesthetized state and receives your acquiescence, she'll inject a paralytic drug to stop the heart. Death is peaceful, painless, and loving.

Euthanasia is an awesome and difficult decision to make, even when circumstances clearly identify it as a kindness. Our pets cannot verbalize their wishes on the subject, and especially eager-to-please Boxers often endure chronic pain or poor quality of life because they sense how much their humans don't want to let go.

The Right Time?

It's not always easy to determine how an animal feels. If your dog has had surgery or broken a limb, it's a fair assumption that he'll experience some pain afterward. A Boxer who experiences sudden pain may yelp in response. A Boxer who has stepped on a sharp object may avoid using the affected paw. But a Boxer experiencing malaise or discomfort from a covert source like an undiagnosed disease may not exhibit clear indications. Dogs are much more stoic about pain than we are, and often endure it quietly. So how do we determine the proper time to let them go? One sign is when your dog has stopped eating or drinking for several days. This is a natural part of the dying process, in which the body prepares to shut down. The dog does not experience discomfort from hunger or thirst the way a healthy animal would. Continuous panting, another indicator, may stem from anxiety or elevated body temperature.

If pain cannot be alleviated and/or a debilitating condition remedied, allowing the dog to live with it is unfair. Is there ever a circumstance in which a dog can die naturally? Of course. But if death doesn't happen during sleep, it may be accompanied by anxiety and/or discomfort. Why subject an ill dog to that when you can ensure a peaceful, painless passage? We owe it to our pets to end their suffering if we cannot ease it.

Euthanasia should never be viewed as a solution to the extra care, special needs, or otherwise inconvenient requirements of a physically challenged or terminally ill pet who can still enjoy a decent quality of life. Only the most selfish of owners would elect to euthanize then. If you can't afford the costs associated with a special-needs dog, ask your vet about any resources that may be able to help pet owners with financial hardship.

HOSPICE

More difficult is the situation in which a pet is not in pain but is not enjoying much quality of life. This is often the case with degenerative myelopathy (DM), a progressive neurological disease often seen in Boxers that ultimately renders their back legs paralyzed. Victims of DM may be perfectly sound in every other way

Multi-Dog Tip

Do not believe the myth that advises euthanizing healthy surviving pets because they can't cope with the loss of a recently deceased pet or owner. Every animal grieves differently. If your surviving dog is mourning the loss of a beloved friend, give him the same love and patience you'd offer any grieving family member.

but can no longer stand up without assistance. Incontinence often develops in the latter stages of the disease, and the leg muscles atrophy from inactivity. There is no cure for this insidious disease, but hospice care can help cope with it and other conditions like it.

The word "hospice" originally referred to lodging available to religious pilgrims and the destitute, usually maintained by monastic orders. Today, hospice refers to a program of palliative care for terminally ill (when death is expected in approximately six months or less) patients and their families. Most hospice patients remain in their own homes, but some hospices have facilities to house terminal patients with no support system.

Hospice care of pets differs from hospice care of humans in that the pet's death is not necessarily imminent, but nursing care is necessary, as in the case of DM and other physical challenges. Wheelcarts and special leashes developed to restore mobility and quality of life to DM victims offer owners a welcome alternative to euthanasia, but not every dog successfully adapts to these devices. Stoicism notwithstanding, is an afflicted Boxer then finding any pleasure in daily life? Is he

Dog hospice refers to a program of palliative care for terminally ill Boxers and other breeds.

content just to exist with you, even though he cannot move about freely or comfortably? These are difficult questions when we know that a truthful answer is often the first step toward letting go of our faithful friends.

PLANNING AHEAD

Although planning a pet's funeral is not as elaborate as that for a human, there are still decisions to be made and steps to take. It is much better to consider these issues long before you need to act. Mourning your beloved Boxer is hard enough without the added pressure of logistics.

Where?

If you anticipate having to euthanize your Boxer, consider where it will take place. Euthanasia performed in an animal hospital is typically very compassionate and respectful. Veterinary offices provide privacy, comfort, and dignity to both owner and pet, but this option nonetheless involves an excursion that may stress the pet, especially if the owner is very emotional or nervous. Many veterinarians will come to the dog's home to administer medications in the comfort of familiar surroundings, or if the dog is in too much pain to be moved. No matter where it takes place, remember that dogs are incredibly sensitive to our feelings. They will detect your agitation and infer that something stressful is about to happen. Try to maintain a calm demeanor if you want to be present during euthanasia.

Body Disposition

Pets have become so important in our lives that we can plan for their final rest as carefully as we do any human loved one. Pet funeral homes, where you can arrange a viewing and memorial service, are increasingly available. Small companies that offer services typically rendered by human funeral homes, such as retrieval of the body or delivery of the ashes, have been established by people who care as much as we do about preserving the dignity of our pets. Private facilities that cremate humans may also cremate pets, and individual cremations typically cost more than mass cremations. Pet cemeteries abound, offering the same comfort to mourners who wish to have closure and a quiet place to visit and remember their pets.

Reputable veterinary practices are as concerned as pet owners to ensure the disposition of deceased pets with the utmost compassion and dignity. Some animal hospitals have their own crematorium on the premises. Veterinary practices often have arrangements with crematoria to dispose of pets whose owners choose not to or haven't the emotional strength to make private arrangements for disposition. If the owners don't find comfort in retaining the ashes of their pet, many crematoria will scatter them in the facility's pet cemetery.

Many families opt to bury their deceased pets on their property and conduct their own funerals. If this idea appeals to you, check with your local government about any prohibitive legislation.

Only you will know if or when getting another dog is right for you.

If you have other dogs, they may have a reaction to the loss of their canine buddy.

GRIEF

No matter the circumstances, losing a pet brings a grief like no other. You've lost a cherished family member, but you live in a society that, for the most part, doesn't equate the death of a pet to the death of a human. Lucky pet owners have a support system of like-minded people who understand the depth of such sorrow. Even luckier are grieving pet owners whose support systems include their boss, employees, clergy, neighbors, and friends who reach out to accommodate your loss.

Children

Most likely, you are not the only family member to be mourning the loss of your pet. How do you explain pet loss to young children? Honesty is always the best policy, in terms that your child can understand. Children intuit unusual happenings and can understand, often at a surprisingly young age, that the family dog was very old or sick and went to another, perhaps more spiritual place, depending on your beliefs. There are many story books on pet loss that you can read with your child to explain the process and instigate a dialogue. If you're an atheist or agnostic and need guidance on explaining death to children, there are resources to help.

Other Pets

If you have other pets, take note of their reactions to the loss. Some pets, especially other dogs, may become very depressed, obviously grieving for their lost friend. Other pets may have enjoyed a perfectly amiable relationship with the deceased but aren't particularly affected by his loss.

Pets mourning other pets can experience many of the same reactions as humans: They sleep more, they lose interest in favorite activities, and they may lose their appetite. Grief must run its own course. The best way to help your pets mourn the loss of another pet is with patience and love, just as you'd treat any other family member. There is no concrete remedy, and you'll receive a lot of unsolicited advice from people: Get a new puppy right away, wait a year before getting a new puppy, adopt a dog around the same age as the pet who's grieving, don't get another dog of the same breed, etc. You know your pets better than anyone does. Go with your instincts. Include your remaining pets in considering any family decisions on future pets. Your happiness is directly proportional to your Boxer's happiness, and vice versa.

Want to Know More?

If and when you're ready to add a new dog to your home, see Chapter 2: Finding and Prepping for Your Puppy or Chapter 5: Finding Your Adult Boxer for some pointers.

50 FUN FACTS EVERY BOXER OWNER SHOULD KNOW

1. Boxers curl their bodies into a "C" shape (perhaps propelled by high-velocity tail wagging?) when happy or excited.

2. Boxers play games by themselves: barking and play bowing to chew bones; standing under large, leafy houseplants and acting surprised at the touch of the leaves; and tossing tennis balls up in the air and chasing them when they land.

3. Boxers groom themselves like cats.

4. Boxers think they are lap dogs.

5. Boxers are high-energy dogs who need regular, vigorous activity.

6. Boxers require minimal grooming.

7. Boxers are naturally inquisitive.

8. Boxers may have fewer dominance issues in two-Boxer homes if they are of opposite genders.

9. Ear-cropping is illegal in most European countries.

10. A Boxer slightly dragging a back paw as he walks may be symptomatic of degenerative myelopathy.

11. Boxers come in two official colors: fawn and brindle (black stripes on a fawn background).

12. White Boxers are technically ultra-flashy fawn Boxers.

13. Boxers lack the gene responsible for black coat coloration; therefore, Boxers touted as "black" are either reverse brindle (extensive black striping that gives the illusion of fawn stripes on a black background) or a mixed breed.

14. Boxers are born jumpers who have been known to jump over 6-foot-high (2-m) fences.

15. Approximately 20 percent of white Boxers are born deaf.

16. The Boxer breed originated in Germany.

17. The average life span of a Boxer is nine to eleven years.

18. The Boxer is the seventh most popular dog breed in the United States.

19. The American Kennel Club (AKC) registered the first Boxer in 1904.

20. The Boxer is one of the "Bully Breeds," the unofficial name of the various dog breeds who originated from the Molossian dogs of ancient civilization.

21. The Boxer is sometimes included in anti-breed legislation because of the breed's roots in fighting and baiting.

22. The AKC classifies the Boxer breed in the Working Group.

23. The United Kennel Club (UKC) classifies the Boxer breed in the Guardian Group.

24. Boxers are born with long, slender tails that are commonly docked to a few inches (cm) within a few days after birth.

25. The practice of ear cropping originated in the dog-fighting culture and served two purposes: 1) to give the dog a more intimidating appearance and 2) to prevent the messy, bloody injuries of torn ears during fights.

26. Boxers have a particular fondness for children.

27. Boxers are not excessive barkers.

28. Boxers often snore.

29. White Boxers are disqualified by the

AKC from conformation showing but are eligible for obedience showing.

30. Boxers are extremely affectionate.

31. Boxers are messy water drinkers because of their long upper lip.

32. Boxers are famous for flatulence.

33. The Boxer's undershot jaw allowed him to maintain a bite hold on a prey animal and still breathe freely.

34. German and English Boxers tend to be larger boned, more heavily muscled, have a broader head, and have a shorter muzzle than US Boxers.

35. Boxers have very expressive eyes.

36. Boxer puppies should not be removed from their mother prior to eight weeks of age.

37. The Boxer's short coat and lean physique make him sensitive to hot and cold climates.

38. The Boxer is a brachycephalic breed, meaning he has a wide head and short muzzle.

39. Boston Terriers are sometimes erroneously called "Miniature Boxers;" purebred Boxers are one standard size.

40. Boxers are naturally curious and will follow your every step.

41. The Boxer in conformation competition may not have white markings that total more than one third of the entire coat.

42. The Boxer's natural ears have only been allowed in US conformation since 2005.

43. In 2008, Bavaria's Heartbreaker became the first natural-eared Boxer to win first place at an American Boxer Club (ABC) show.

44. The Boxer is considered deep-chested, meaning the length of the chest from the backbone to sternum is long and the width of the chest is narrower.

45. Ch. Bang Away of Sirrah's Crest is the "winningest" Boxer of all time, winning 121 all-breed Best in Show titles, siring 81 US champion Boxers, and siring 7 ABC-designated Sires/Dams of Merit.

46. White Boxers were used in Germany for police night work until it was discovered that their white coloration was too visible.

47. The source of the name "Boxer" is unclear, but popular belief says that it came from the dog's use of his front paws in a "boxing" manner during play. It's unlikely, though, that Germany would name its proud new dog breed after a British national symbol like boxing.

48. The Boxer is tenacious and independent thinking.

49. Between 1919 and 1924, no Boxers at all were registered with the AKC.

50. The Boxer served Germany in both World Wars, acting as couriers, guards in POW camps, detecting the enemy on the front lines, identifying smugglers in and out of the country, acting as ambulance dogs, and detecting mustard gas and incoming mortar shells.

RESOURCES

ASSOCIATIONS AND ORGANIZATIONS

Breed Clubs

American Boxer Club (ABC)
http://americanboxerclub.org

American Kennel Club (AKC)
5580 Centerview Drive
Raleigh, NC 27606
Telephone: (919) 233-9767
Fax: (919) 233-3627
E-Mail: info@akc.org
www.akc.org

Boxer Club of Canada Inc.
http://boxerclubofcanada.com/

Canadian Kennel Club (CKC)
89 Skyway Avenue, Suite 100
Etobicoke, Ontario M9W 6R4
Telephone: (416) 675-5511
Fax: (416) 675-6506
E-Mail: information@ckc.ca
www.ckc.ca

Federation Cynologique
Internationale (FCI)
Secretariat General de la FCI
Place Albert 1er, 13
B – 6530 Thuin
Belqique
www.fci.be
The British Boxer Club
|www.thebritishboxerclub.co.uk

The Kennel Club
1 Clarges Street
London
W1J 8AB
Telephone: 0870 606 6750
Fax: 0207 518 1058
www.the-kennel-club.org.uk

United Kennel Club (UKC)
100 E. Kilgore Road
Kalamazoo, MI 49002-5584
Telephone: (269) 343-9020
Fax: (269) 343-7037
E-Mail: pbickell@ukcdogs.com
www.ukcdogs.com

Pet Sitters

National Association of
Professional Pet Sitters
15000 Commerce Parkway,
Suite C
Mt. Laurel, New Jersey 08054
Telephone: (856) 439-0324
Fax: (856) 439-0525
E-Mail: napps@ahint.com
www.petsitters.org

Pet Sitters International
201 East King Street
King, NC 27021-9161
Telephone: (336) 983-9222
Fax: (336) 983-5266
E-Mail: info@petsit.com
www.petsit.com

Rescue Organizations and Animal Welfare Groups

American Humane
Association (AHA)
63 Inverness Drive East
Englewood, CO 80112
Telephone: (303) 792-9900
Fax: 792-5333
www.americanhumane.org

American Society for the
Prevention of Cruelty to
Animals (ASPCA)
424 E. 92nd Street
New York, NY 10128-6804
Telephone: (212) 876-7700
www.aspca.org

The Humane Society of the
United States (HSUS)
2100 L Street, NW
Washington DC 20037
Telephone: (202) 452-1100
www.hsus.org

Royal Society for the
Prevention of Cruelty to
Animals (RSPCA)
RSPCA Enquiries Service
Wilberforce Way, Southwater,
Horsham, West Sussex RH13
9RS
United Kingdom
Telephone: 0870 3335 999
Fax: 0870 7530 284
www.rspca.org.uk

Sports

International Agility Link (IAL)
Global Administrator: Steve Drinkwater
E-Mail: yunde@powerup.au
www.agilityclick.com/~ial

The World Canine Freestyle Organization, Inc.
P.O. Box 350122
Brooklyn, NY 11235
Telephone: (718) 332-8336
Fax: (718) 646-2686
E-Mail: WCFODOGS@aol.com
www.worldcaninefreestyle.org

Therapy

Delta Society
875 124th Ave, NE, Suite 101
Bellevue, WA 98005
Telephone: (425) 679-5500
Fax: (425) 679-5539
E-Mail: info@DeltaSociety.org
www.deltasociety.org

Therapy Dogs Inc.
P.O. Box 20227
Cheyenne WY 82003
Telephone: (877) 843-7364
Fax: (307) 638-2079
E-Mail: therapydogsinc@qwestoffice.net
www.therapydogs.com

Therapy Dogs International (TDI)
88 Bartley Road
Flanders, NJ 07836
Telephone: (973) 252-9800
Fax: (973) 252-7171
E-Mail: tdi@gti.net
www.tdi-dog.org

Training

Association of Pet Dog Trainers (APDT)
150 Executive Center Drive
Box 35
Greenville, SC 29615
Telephone: (800) PET-DOGS
Fax: (864) 331-0767
E-Mail: information@apdt.com
www.apdt.com

International Association of Animal Behavior Consultants (IAABC)
565 Callery Road
Cranberry Township, PA 16066
E-Mail: info@iaabc.org
www.iaabc.org

National Association of Dog Obedience Instructors (NADOI)
PMB 369
729 Grapevine Hwy.
Hurst, TX 76054-2085
www.nadoi.org

Veterinary and Health Resources

Academy of Veterinary Homeopathy (AVH)
P.O. Box 9280
Wilmington, DE 19809
Telephone: (866) 652-1590
Fax: (866) 652-1590
www.theavh.org

American Academy of Veterinary Acupuncture (AAVA)
P.O. Box 1058
Glastonbury, CT 06033
Telephone: (860) 632-9911
Fax: (860) 659-8772
www.aava.org

American Animal Hospital Association (AAHA)
12575 W. Bayaud Ave.
Lakewood, CO 80228
Telephone: (303) 986-2800
Fax: (303) 986-1700
E-Mail: info@aahanet.org
www.aahanet.org/index.cfm

American College of Veterinary Internal Medicine (ACVIM)
1997 Wadsworth Blvd.

Suite A
Lakewood, CO 80214-5293
Telephone: (800) 245-9081
Fax: (303) 231-0880
Email: ACVIM@ACVIM.org
www.acvim.org

American College of Veterinary Ophthalmologists (ACVO)
P.O. Box 1311
Meridian, ID 83860
Telephone: (208) 466-7624
Fax: (208) 466-7693
E-Mail: office09@acvo.com
www.acvo.com

American Holistic Veterinary Medical Association (AHVMA)
2218 Old Emmorton Road
Bel Air, MD 21015
Telephone: (410) 569-0795
Fax: (410) 569-2346
E-Mail: office@ahvma.org
www.ahvma.org

American Veterinary Medical Association (AVMA)
1931 North Meacham Road, Suite 100
Schaumburg, IL 60173-4360
Telephone: (847) 925-8070
Fax: (847) 925-1329
E-Mail: avmainfo@avma.org
www.avma.org

ASPCA Animal Poison Control Center
Telephone: (888) 426-4435
www.aspca.org

British Veterinary Association (BVA)
7 Mansfield Street
London
W1G 9NQ
Telephone: 0207 636 6541
Fax: 0207 908 6349
E-Mail: bvahq@bva.co.uk
www.bva.co.uk

Canine Eye Registration Foundation (CERF)
VMDB/CERF
1717 Philo Rd
P O Box 3007
Urbana, IL 61803-3007
Telephone: (217) 693-4800
Fax: (217) 693-4801
E-Mail: CERF@vmbd.org
www.vmdb.org

Orthopedic Foundation for Animals (OFA)
2300 NE Nifong Blvd
Columbus, Missouri 65201-3856
Telephone: (573) 442-0418
Fax: (573) 875-5073
Email: ofa@offa.org
www.offa.org

US Food and Drug Administration Center for Veterinary Medicine (CVM)
7519 Standish Place
HFV-12
Rockville, MD 20855-0001
Telephone: (240) 276-9300
or (888) INFO-FDA
http://www.fda.gov/cvm

PUBLICATIONS

BOOKS

Anderson, Teoti. *The Super Simple Guide to Housetraining*. Neptune City: TFH Publications, 2004.

Anne, Jonna, with Mary Straus. *The Healthy Dog Cookbook: 50 Nutritious and Delicious Recipes Your Dog Will Love*. UK: Ivy Press Limited, 2008.

Boneham, Sheila Webster, Ph.D. *The Boxer*. Neptune City: TFH Publications, 2005.

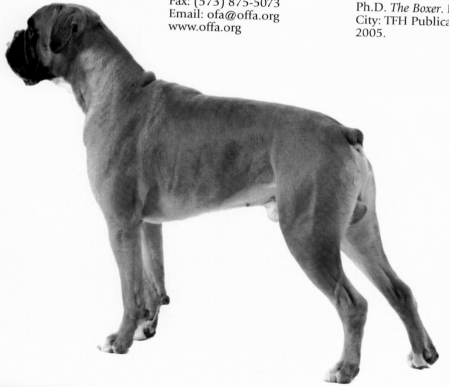

Dainty, Suellen. *50 Games to Play With Your Dog*. UK: Ivy Press Limited, 2007.

Gallagher, Cynthia P. *Boxers*. Neptune City: TFH Publications and Discovery Communications, Inc., 2006.

Morgan, Diane. *Good Dogkeeping*. Neptune City: TFH Publications, 2005.

MAGAZINES
AKC Family Dog
American Kennel Club
260 Madison Avenue
New York, NY 10016
Telephone: (800) 490-5675
E-Mail: familydog@akc.org
www.akc.org/pubs/familydog

AKC Gazette
American Kennel Club
260 Madison Avenue
New York, NY 10016
Telephone: (800) 533-7323
E-Mail: gazette@akc.org
www.akc.org/pubs/gazette

Dog & Kennel
Pet Publishing, Inc.
7-L Dundas Circle
Greensboro, NC 27407
Telephone: (336) 292-4272
Fax: (336) 292-4272
E-Mail: info@petpublishing.com
www.dogandkennel.com

Dogs Monthly
Ascot House
High Street, Ascot,
Berkshire SL5 7JG
United Kingdom
Telephone: 0870 730 8433
Fax: 0870 730 8431
E-Mail: admin@rtc-associates.freeserve.co.uk
www.corsini.co.uk/dogsmonthly

WEBSITES
Nylabone
www.nylabone.com

TFH Publications, Inc.
www.tfh.com

PHOTO CREDITS

Angela kay Agnew (Shutterstock): 132

Art_man (Shutterstock): 131, 220

Joy Brown (Shutterstock): 92

cabania (Shutterstock): 190

Diego Cervo (Shutterstock): 57

cynoclub (Shutterstock): 18, 22, 64

Waldemar Dabrowski (Shutterstock): 121

Tad Denson (Shutterstock): 74, 75

epromocja (Shutterstock): 1

Ken Drori (Shutterstock): 200

Guilu (Shutterstock): 80, 212

Karen Givens (Shutterstock): 84, 90, 101, 111, 118, 138, 142

Vladimir Gramagin (Shutterstock): 209

Nelson Hale (Shutterstock): 202

Margo Harrison (Shutterstock): 6

Jostein Hauge (Shutterstock): 120, 129

Garth Helms (Shutterstock): 100

Jerry Horbert (Shutterstock): 169

Dee Hunter (Shutterstock): 9, 174 (bottom)

Eric Isselée (Shutterstock): 15, 19, 43, 61, 76, 166, 173 (dog), 192, 206, 218

Peter Kim (Shutterstock): 104

Christophe Konfortion (Shutterstock): 78 (bottom), 82, 108

Erik Lam (Shutterstock): 11, 17, 35, 89, 117, 154, 195, 203, 211

michael ledray (Shutterstock): 158, 214

George Lee (Shutterstock): 34, 36, 41, 115, 144, 150, 172

Donald Linscott (Shutterstock): 162

Naturespixel (Shutterstock): 62

Adam Majchrzak (Shutterstock): 124

mjt (Shutterstock): 98, 205

Selyutina Olga (Shutterstock): 66

Mikhail Olykainen (Shutterstock): 175, 193

Regien Paassen (Shutterstock): 123

James Peragine (Shutterstock): 125

Draper photography (Shutterstock): 79

Michael Felix Photography (Shutterstock): 88

Morgan Lane Photography (Shutterstock): 24

South 12th Photography (Shutterstock): 94

inacio pires (Shutterstock): 110, 216

Jessie Eldora Robertson (Shutterstock): 160

Anna Sedneva (Shutterstock): 178

Eremin Sergey (Shutterstock): 176

Shutterstock (Shutterstock): 8, 44, 86, 140

Dwight Smith (Shutterstock): 155

SueC (Shutterstock): 136

Sherrianne Talon (Shutterstock): cover, 78 (top), 156

Stana (Shutterstock): 96, 106

K. Thorsen (Shutterstock): 27

Zoran Tripalo (Shutterstock): 148

April Turner (Shutterstock): 184

Lebedinski Vladislav (Shutterstock): 107, 208

Stas Volik (Shutterstock): 114

Aleksandar Vozarevic (Shutterstock): 52

All other photos courtesy of Isabelle Francais and TFH archives

DEDICATION

ABOUT THE AUTHOR

Cynthia P. Gallagher lives in Annapolis, Maryland, with her husband and Boxer. A member of the Dog Writers Association of America (DWAA), she is the author of five single-breed dog books. Visit her on the web at www.cynthiapgallagher.com.

VETERINARY ADVISOR

Wayne Hunthausen, DVM, consulting veterinary editor and pet behavior consultant, is the director of Animal Behavior Consultations in the Kansas City area and currently serves on the Practitioner Board for *Veterinary Medicine* and the Behavior Advisory Board for *Veterinary Forum*.

BREEDER ADVISOR

Lee Morris has been breeding and showing since 1972 under the Katandy prefix with numerous Champions, mostly Boxers. She also bred the Winners Dog and Best of Winners at the American Boxer Club National Specialty in 2008, Ch Katandy's Fast Forward. She resides in Davidsonville, Maryland, with her husband and family of dogs. Visit her website at www.katandyboxers.com .